"Unbaptized adults often share their catechesis and ritual plan with people baptized in other Christian denominations East and West. Some initiation ministers naively fail to distinguish these groups. This book provides a comprehensive history of these practices and of their assumptions. Readers will appreciate anew the subtle yet important distinctions among those who seek reception into the full communion of the Catholic Church."

—Paul Turner, author of *Sacred Times*

"The tension between official recognition of baptism across Catholic, Orthodox, and Protestant communions and local rites of membership reception bedevils the work for Christian unity. Through careful study of the Christian tradition's posture toward heretics, schismatics, and penitents, the authors uncover the historical, liturgical, and theological roots of this tension, and point to a healing path forward. *One Baptism—One Church?* offers hopeful practices for ecumenical dreamers."

—Edgardo A. Colón-Emeric, dean of
the Duke University Divinity School

# One Baptism—One Church?

*A History and Theology
of the Reception of Baptized Christians*

Kimberly Hope Belcher, Nathan P. Chase,
and Alexander Turpin

LITURGICAL PRESS
ACADEMIC

Collegeville, Minnesota
litpress.org

**Library of Congress Cataloging-in-Publication Data**

Names: Belcher, Kimberly Hope, author. | Chase, Nathan, author. | Turpin, Alexander (Alexander T.), author.
Title: One baptism-one church? : a history and theology of the reception of baptized Christians / Kimberly Hope Belcher, Nathan P. Chase, and Alexander Turpin.
Description: Collegeville, Minnesota : Liturgical Press Academic, [2024] | Includes index. | Summary: "Over the centuries Christians have recognized the baptism of those outside their own ecclesial body, but the practices of receiving those who are already baptized from other groups proclaim social, theological, and ecclesial distinctions. How do contemporary practices reflect theological principles and historical development? One Baptism-One Church? demonstrates how the social context and organization of local communities leads to prioritizing inner coherence and security over theological principles"— Provided by publisher.
Identifiers: LCCN 2024017251 (print) | LCCN 2024017252 (ebook) | ISBN 9780814689127 (trade paperback) | ISBN 9780814689134 (epub) | ISBN 9780814689141 (pdf)
Subjects: LCSH: Catholic Church—Reception of baptized Christians—History. | Baptism and Christian union.
Classification: LCC BX2045.R383 B45 2024  (print) | LCC BX2045.R383  (ebook) | DDC 234/.161—dc23/ eng/20240610
LC record available at https://lccn.loc.gov/2024017251
LC ebook record available at https://lccn.loc.gov/2024017252

# Contents

# Acknowledgments

We are grateful to Stefanos Alexopoulos, Yury Avvakumov, James Bradley, Harald Buchinger, Brian Butcher, Paul Elhallal, Daniel Galadza, Lizette Larson-Miller, Tom McLean, Scott Moore, Anna Petrin, Gregory Shokhikyan, and Karen Westerfield Tucker for their comments on our sources and on various contemporary practices. We also acknowledge our debt to those who attended our presentation at Societas Liturgica in Maynooth, Ireland, in August 2023 and assisted us with their attention, questions, and comments.

# Abbreviations

| | |
|---|---|
| BELS | Bibliotheca Ephemerides Liturgicae, Subsidia |
| CCCOGD | Corpus Christianorum Conciliorum Oecumenicorum Generaliumque Decreta |
| CCSL | Corpus Christianorum, Series Latina |
| CSEL | Corpus Scriptorum Ecclesiasticorum Latinorum |
| GCS | *Die Griechischen christlichen Schriftsteller der ersten Jahrhunderte* |
| LG | *Lumen Gentium* |
| LO | *Liber Ordinum* |
| OCA | Orthodox Church in America |
| OCIA | *Order of Christian Initiation of Adults* |
| PG | Patrologia Graeca |
| PL | Patrologia Latina |
| PRG | Romano-Germanic Pontifical |
| PWD | Pontifical of William Durandus |

| | |
|---|---|
| RCIA | *Rite of Christian Initiation of Adults* |
| ROCOR | Russian Orthodox Church Outside of Russia |
| SC | Sources chrétiennes |
| UR | *Unitatis Redintegratio* |
| USCCB | United States Conference of Catholic Bishops |

Chapter One

# Ecumenism and the Reception
# of Christians from Other Churches

## Introduction

The rite of reception of baptized Christians, currently part of the new *Order of Christian Initiation of Adults*, plays a very important pastoral purpose for Christians who, for a variety of reasons, are entering the Roman Catholic Church. The rite also expresses (even if not always intentionally) convictions about the traditions from which candidates come. For example, imagine three candidates entering the Roman Catholic Church from the Anglican, mainline Protestant, and Evangelical traditions. One might be joining because they have come to intellectually accept some Catholic doctrine or practice that was absent (or not clearly taught) in their prior tradition, or because they are rejecting something about their previous tradition. Another was baptized as a child or adolescent but has not regularly attended worship or faith formation. A third is a regular practitioner in another community but wishes to become Catholic for the sake of family unity with a Catholic parent, spouse, or child. The current ritual for receiving these baptized Christians

1

includes a private reconciliation sometime before confirmation and a Mass that includes confirmation followed by First Communion. Often, confirmation and Communion are given at the Easter Vigil, although there are other options in the liturgical book. For each of these three candidates, these rites negotiate their understanding of their past religious history quite differently, even if the rites are identical. In addition to its personal meaning, the performance of these rites also expresses something about the Catholic Church's understanding of these communities. Sometimes, the practices seem to be at odds with what the Catholic Church teaches in its documents about these communities and their relationship to the Catholic Church.

The Second Vatican Council's Decree on Ecumenism (*Unitatis Redintegratio*, henceforth UR) in 1964, for example, is already very clear that baptized Christians coming into full communion with the Catholic Church are not penitents: "One cannot charge with the sin of the separation those who at present are born into these communities and in them are brought up in the faith of Christ, and the Catholic Church accepts them with respect and affection as brothers. For [those] who believe in Christ and have been properly baptized are put in some, though imperfect, communion with the Catholic Church."[1] In pastoral practice, however, having reconciliation be their first sacramental ministry from the Catholic Church seems to imply that their separation is a sin, even a grave one. This is especially true for a

---

1. Vatican II, Decree on Ecumenism (*Unitatis Redintegratio*), 3, in *Vatican Council II: The Conciliar and Postconciliar Documents*, ed. Austin Flannery (Collegeville, MN: Liturgical Press, 2014).

candidate who comes rejecting what they believe is the doctrine and practice of their church of origin, whose doubts are then amplified and aired by the sacramental progression of reconciliation-confirmation-Communion.

The reception of baptized Christians from other communions manifests the Catholic Church's understanding of the boundaries of the church. On the one hand, mutual recognition of baptism and agreements on doctrine have significantly eased pastoral care for the reception of baptized Christians, but on the other hand, the rituals for this transition risk creating more distance between the Catholic Church and other Christian communities than is theologically justified. The introduction to the current rite of reception says, "[T]hose aspects that in any way have an air of triumphalism should be carefully avoided. . . . Consideration must be given both to the good of ecumenism and to the bond between the candidate and the parish community."[2] A second tension in actual liturgical practice emerges because documents like this are promulgated from offices that are strongly committed to ecumenism, but their implementation is the work of ministers that may not be well formed in ecumenism or ecclesiology (or, for that matter, liturgy).[3] In pastoral practice, then, the tension may be between pastoral care and a kind of Catholic triumphalism instead of between that care and ecumenical commitments. Often,

---

2. *Order of Christian Initiation of Adults* (OCIA) (Collegeville, MN: Liturgical Press, 2024), 475b.

3. Pontifical Council for Promoting Christian Unity, *Directory for the Application of Principles and Norms on Ecumenism* (Vatican City: Libreria Editrice Vaticana, 1993), 77–86, calls for ecumenical education for ministers, but this is very unevenly attained.

Christians who come seeking full communion wish to reject their own ecclesial history, which increases the triumphal pressure on ministers and peers.

## "One Lord, One Faith, One Baptism"

The mutual recognition of baptism has been a benchmark and foundation stone for ecumenical efforts, not only in the Roman Catholic Church but more broadly. Expanding on the "one body and one Spirit, just as you were called to the one hope of your calling; one Lord, one faith, one Baptism" of Ephesians 4:4-6, UR proclaimed for Roman Catholics that "all who have been justified by faith in baptism are incorporated into Christ; they therefore have a right to be called Christians, and with good reason are accepted as brothers [and sisters] by the children of the Catholic Church" (UR 3; see also *Lumen Gentium* 15). Similarly commenting on Ephesians 4, the World Council of Churches' Faith and Order Commission's 1982 convergence document *Baptism, Eucharist and Ministry* comments, "Through baptism, Christians are brought into union with Christ, with each other and with the Church of every time and place. Our common baptism, which unites us to Christ in faith, is thus a basic bond of unity. We are one people and are called to confess and serve one Lord in each place and in all the world."[4] The first document of the international dialogue between Rome and the united Eastern Orthodox Churches (1982) treats the foundational character

4. World Council of Churches, Faith and Order Commission, *Baptism, Eucharist and Ministry (Faith and Order Paper No. 111, the "Lima Text")* (Geneva: World Council of Churches, 1982), §6.

of baptism for Christian unity: "The body of Christ is unique. There exists then only one church of God. The identity of one eucharistic assembly with another comes from the fact that all with the same faith celebrate the same memorial, that all by eating the same bread and sharing in the same cup become the same unique body of Christ into which they have been integrated by the same baptism."[5] The same thing can be seen in numerous bilateral documents, each of which makes the point that recognizing one another as part of the universal church and the one Body of Christ begins in a shared recognition of one another's baptism.

Christians move toward unity not only by sharing the theology of baptism, but also by respecting one another's baptismal practice. For instance, the joint declaration issued by Pope Francis of Rome and Pope Tawadros II of Cairo in 2017 suggests a step toward better ecumenical relations between the Roman Catholic and the Coptic Orthodox Church:

> The bond uniting us was received from our one Lord on the day of our Baptism. . . . Today we, Pope Francis and Pope Tawadros II, in order to please the heart of the Lord Jesus, as well as that of our sons and daughters in the faith, mutually declare that we, with one mind and heart, will seek sincerely not to repeat the baptism that has

---

5. Joint Commission for Theological Dialogue Between the Roman Catholic Church and the Orthodox Church, "The Mystery of the Church and of the Eucharist in the Light of the Mystery of the Holy Trinity" (Vatican City: Pontifical Council for Promoting Christian Unity, 1982), III.1.

> been administered in either of our Churches for
> any person who wishes to join the other.[6]

We may think of this ecumenical concern as a modern one, but as we will argue, the early Christian consensus on the unrepeatability of baptism was linked from its origins to recognizing the genuine initiation into Jesus Christ, even of groups that were considered heretical or schismatic.

Already in the third century, "one Lord, one faith, one baptism" provided the foundation for determining what should be considered a genuine baptism. Tertullian (c. 155–220 CE[7]), for instance, argued "the one Lord, one God, and one faith could be found only within the one, true church; the one baptism could not be separated from one Christ, God, church, and faith."[8] This gave grounds for ruling out the baptism of "heretics" (groups divided by significant theological differences, generally regarding the Trinity or the natures of Christ). Cyprian (c. 210–258), on the other hand, stressed the Holy Spirit's power to forgive sins, which could only come through the ministry of a true bishop.[9] This put "schismatics" (in the East: including heresies not related to trinitarian doctrine; in the West: those who owe allegiance to false hierarchs) outside

6. Pope Francis and Pope Tawadros II, "Joint Declaration Pope Francis and Pope Tawadros" (Cairo: Coptic Orthodox Patriarchate, 2017), 4, 11.

7. All dates are from the Common Era.

8. J. Patout Burns, "Baptism as Dying and Rising with Christ in the Teaching of Augustine," *Journal of Early Christian Studies* 20, no. 3 (2012): 421.

9. Burns, "Baptism," 421.

the range of the true church that could offer the "one baptism."[10] In the fourth and fifth centuries, the Donatist controversy, in turn, raised questions about the baptism of "apostates" (former members who left due to persecution or conversion to a competing faith).

Today, these categories seem at odds with church teaching that those who have been properly baptized have the right to be called Christians (UR 3).[11] Instead, we will use the modern and ecumenical terminology "baptized Christians." In so doing we also turn the ancient debate over Ephesians 4 on its head: if we can recognize one baptism for those we receive into full communion, can we not also grow into a greater communion with their communities of origin?[12] Can the sacramental incorporation of these baptized Christians witness also to the light of Christ that they received at their baptism and that they continue to bear?

10. The patristic and Byzantine texts—whether liturgical, theological, or canonical—never use the word "convert." Instead, they talk about, e.g., "how to receive those turning away from heresy." So, for instance, the title of Trullo can. 95: "Περὶ τοῦ πῶς δέχεσθαι τοὺς ἐξ αἱρέσεως ἐπιστρέφοντας." Trullo can. 95, ed. Georges Nedungatt and Silvano Agrestini, CCCOGD 1 (Turnhout: Brepols, 2006), 287.

11. In the Eastern Orthodox churches, "converts" is the term usually used today in official documents and services of reception into Orthodoxy; in the past, the terms "heretics" or "schismatics" were used, and are still used by some communities today.

12. "Growth in communion" here reflects the Lutheran-Roman Catholic Commission on Unity, "Baptism and Growth in Communion" (Lutheran World Federation/Pontifical Council for the Promotion of Christian Unity, 2022).

# Receptive Ecumenism and Growth
# in Communion

Ecumenism is always done from a particular ecclesial location; no Christian has a God's-eye view of the extent and shape of the church. The three of us writing this study write as Roman Catholics, strongly committed to the project of Christian unity. We intend to examine the history and current Roman Catholic practice of the reception of baptized Christians, seeking ways that contemporary practice may be an obstacle to the full expression of our ecumenical commitments and how history can reshape that practice.

Ecumenism is not only a modern project for the reunion of denominations. It is, rather, the recognition of the invisible church of those God has chosen in Christ (the *oikoumene* or universal church). Christians have always recognized in principle that the church of Christ, infused by the Holy Spirit, extends beyond the boundaries of their own communion. The mutual recognition of baptism within the ecumenical movement takes that principle to the practical level by recognizing specific Christian communities as places where the one baptism is bestowed and thus the one church can be found.[13]

---

13. Alluding to *Lumen Gentium* 8, UR 4 refers to the ecumenical movement, by which "little by little, as the obstacles to perfect ecclesiastical communion are overcome, all Christians will be gathered, in a common celebration of the Eucharist, into the unity of the one and only Church, which Christ bestowed on his Church from the beginning. This unity, we believe, subsists in the Catholic Church as something she can never lose, and we hope that it will continue to increase until the end of time." The idea that the unity of Christ's body, the church, "subsists" (*subsistit*) in the Catholic

Receptive ecumenism, an innovative approach to dialogue developed through a series of conferences at Durham University, prioritizes listening to one's dialogue partners and finding estimable parts of their tradition that can be valued, embraced, and received alongside and into one's own ecclesial inheritance.[14] Rather than considering every doctrinal, liturgical, or juridical difference as a threat to church unity, receptive ecumenism presupposes that certain types of diversity may be legitimate or even received as a gift by the universal church of Christ.[15] In studying the reception of baptized Christians, we see two ways receptive ecumenism can contribute. On the one hand, Christians who are received into communion with Rome bring with them gifts received from their community of origin and often from other traditions as well. It is an ecumenical act, then, to value the formation of our candidates for full communion, and if need be to witness to that value for them and their families

---

Church privileges the Catholic communion as a visible witness to ecclesial unity but refuses to strictly identify the "Catholic Church" with the fullness of the Body of Christ. The best way of interpreting *subsistit* is still under ecumenical discussion, but it is clear from this passage both that the Catholic Church is understood to possess that unity and that this unity is incomplete.

14. Receptive ecumenism has currently been explored through seven projects at the University of Durham: https://www.durham .ac.uk/research/institutes-and-centres/catholic-studies/research /constructive-catholic-theology-/receptive-ecumenism-/.

15. Kimberly Hope Belcher, *Eucharist and Receptive Ecumenism: From Thanksgiving to Communion* (Cambridge/New York: Cambridge University Press, 2020).

and friends.[16] On the other hand, the historical practice and theological interpretation of the reception of baptized Christians can constructively critique and reconfigure a contemporary rite that is burdened with a specific, historically limited conception of the sacraments of initiation.

Closely connected to the work of receptive ecumenism is the concept of growth in communion. This approach to ecumenical work is grounded in the recognition of baptism, and thus of church belonging, that spans ecclesial boundaries. Recognition of baptism also implies a communion, even if imperfect, between the Roman Catholic Church and every Christian (UR 3). The challenge of the ecumenical movement, according to the Lutheran-Roman Catholic Commission on Unity's 2022 document, "Baptism and Growth in Communion," is to develop that imperfect communion by recognizing, with the help of the Holy Spirit, the ways that the Body of Christ already exceeds the limit of human perception.

> Since the body of Christ is a reality that transcends denominational divisions, participation in the body of Christ transcends the separation of the churches. The reality of the one body of Christ precedes the churches' efforts to re-establish unity among themselves. . . . Lutherans and Catholics . . . strive to overcome the paradoxical situation that, on the one hand, the baptized are members of the body of Christ and the communities of the

16. See Kimberly Hope Belcher, "Baptized by Christ, Baptized into Christ," presented at Christian Churches Together Forum, "Water that Unites and Water that Divides: Baptism and the Journey to Unity and Reconciliation," Savannah, GA, October 3, 2023.

baptized are also members of the body of Christ and therefore in communion with one another, while, on the other hand, these communities are nevertheless also separated from each other. This painful situation of the one body of Christ, wounded by the lack of full communion of its members, calls for ways to strengthen its growth in communion.[17]

Both growth in communion and receptive ecumenism commit Christians to examine their current practices, including reception of Christians from other communities. Here we seek to remove obstacles to the more complete expression and recognition of Christian unity, as well as for concrete ways that our partial communion could be better expressed.

Since Roman Catholic practices have generally been evaluated for their faithfulness to the historical record, a thorough historical examination is needed. Since Vatican II, the historical evidence from Eastern Christianity has been given significant weight, in addition

17. Lutheran-Roman Catholic Commission on Unity, "Baptism and Growth in Communion," 3.6.5. This approach to ecumenism is a natural development of the documents "on the way" that explicitly describe dialogue documents as milestones to full ecclesial communion; see, e.g., Bishops' Committee for Ecumenical and Interreligious Affairs, USCCB and Evangelical Lutheran Church in America, "Declaration on the Way: Church, Ministry, and Eucharist," 2015, http://www.usccb.org/beliefs-and-teachings/ecumenical -and-interreligious/ecumenical/lutheran/_upload/Declaration_on _the_Way-for-Website.pdf; Anglican–Roman Catholic International Commission III, "Walking Together on the Way: Learning to Be the Church – Local, Regional, Universal" (Erfurt, Germany, 2018), https://iarccum.org/doc/?d=721.

to that from Western historical sources. Too often, explicitly ecumenical studies have focused on official documents issued by central authorities, while evidence from the borderlands contradicts those documents. We have found the contrast between central legislation and peripheral practice between the Eastern and Western churches to be a particularly fruitful area for research.

## The Social Dimensions of Church Communities

"Baptism" in the Eastern churches, and in the Western churches until the disintegration of initiation,[18] included the handlaying and chrism rites known as "chrismation" in the East, as well as similar ceremonies that eventually became known as "confirmation" in the West. Consequently, to profess "one baptism" means also to consider how repetitions of our initiation gestures impede our full recognition of one another's chrismation practice. Confirming Protestants puts some pressure on our assertions that they have been fully initiated; confirmation of Eastern Christians is yet worse. Confirming or rebaptizing validly baptized Eastern Christians is definitely against the Catholic Church's current norms, yet it is easy to find anecdotal examples when it has been done. Why does this happen?

The treatment of "irregularly baptized" Christians demonstrates quite a bit about how churches understand the boundaries of the ecclesial Body of Christ. Theologically speaking, a clearer boundary between the baptized and the unbaptized corresponds with

18. Nathan Mitchell, "Christian Initiation: Decline and Dismemberment," *Worship* 48, no. 8 (October 1974): 458–79.

a conviction that the invisible church, Christ's body, is contiguous with the visible church of those who are recognized members. Understanding baptism as a radical immersion into Christ's living and social body leads to different expectations, and also different treatment, for those who are understood to be Christians and those who are not. Christians could treat those outside the social body who are not behaving as they expect baptized persons to behave (such as heretics, schismatics, and serious sinners) as if they are not baptized. This solution might be cognitively appealing, but it was generally not considered acceptable to early Christians. Rather, schismatic groups and serious sinners were often understood as part of the church in one way and outside it in another. Reception of baptized Christians from so-called "heretical" or "schismatic" groups played a formative role in early Christians' understanding of the boundaries of the church, and the categories generated by early debates continue to be influential today.[19]

Why have different Christian communities felt a need to baptize or anoint, even in situations where their own ecclesiology and legal authorities have recommended, instead, either a profession of faith or simple admission to communion? In the borderlands, especially, where Eastern and Western missionaries were both operating and where the aristocracy was

19. For an introduction to this early conflict about the nature and boundaries of the church and the categories it established, see J. Patout Burns, "On Rebaptism: Social Organization in the Third Century Church," *Journal of Early Christian Studies* 1, no. 4 (Winter 1993): 367–403.

struggling to maintain its social power, Christian history shows local ministers consistently neglecting authoritative commands to recognize the valid baptism of Christians coming from another ecclesial tradition. In that context, ninth- or fifteenth-century Christians, as we will see, assumed that to be a "Latin" was to reject everything that smacked of being "Byzantine." Today, despite a great deal of official ecumenical progress, many Christians feel the same way about the labels "Catholic" and "Protestant." Mary Douglas's cultural theory suggests that rites of reception become an opportunity to strengthen the symbolic opposition between self and other.[20] The person being received, after all, is a potent symbol of their former community, and barriers to their entry or triumphalism in their reception create symbolic distance between the two communities.

When human beings feel threatened by things outside their safe categories, they often express this through their ritual practices. Just as a breach in the skin of the physical body can be a dangerous source of infection, an unregulated opening in the social body often makes members feel vulnerable. This symbolic vulnerability can take the form of either a concern about the fragility of one's personal belonging to the community or of a pervasive disintegration of the symbolic world that helps the entire community understand their world.[21]

20. Mary Douglas, *Natural Symbols: Explorations in Cosmology* (New York: Pantheon Books, 1970); Douglas, *Risk and Blame: Essays in Cultural Theory* (New York: Routledge, 2003).

21. A symbolic world includes perceptions about the natural and supernatural world, including the division of responsibilities

One way to keep each individual transition from feeling like a breach of one's symbolic boundaries is to raise the barriers of entry. Like the body's white blood cells, scrupulous performance of rites of entry clarifies the distinction between the church of origin and the destination, while also serving to "cleanse" the person of the perceived taint of coming from another community.

Rites for bringing in a new member create a sense of the community's outer boundaries by symbolically reflecting these boundaries on the initiate's body. This means that different intensities of ritual performance are interpreted by participants as having different implications about the "wrongness" or distance of the community of origin. Treatment of the boundaries of the human body, skin and orifices, reflects concerns about the boundaries of the social body. Restrictions on eating particular foods or rules for ritual washing often reflect a desire to maintain boundaries around the social community.[22] We would expect, then, that food rites and bathing rites would be those singled out to clarify the ways that Christian belonging does or does not extend beyond a community's borders.

Within the Catholic imagination even to the present day, sacramental relationships, even though spiritual and internal, are closely connected to embodied contact. This can be seen in one way in the longstanding

---

between genders, ages, parents and children, and leaders and followers in society.

22. Mary Douglas, "Deciphering a Meal," *Daedalus* 101, no. 1 (1972): 61–81; cf. Douglas and Baron C. Isherwood, *The World of Goods: Towards an Anthropology of Consumption*, rev. ed. (London/New York: Routledge, 1996).

Western Catholic insistence on the bishop's personal imposition of hands for the sacrament of confirmation, an insistence that, among other things, has produced both internal and external problems—such as how and when to identify "complete" initiation, as well as confusion between confirmation and other liturgies that include the laying on of hands, such as the rite for receiving a validly baptized Christian into full communion.[23] In another way, this sense of physical contact governs our treatment of apostolic succession: ordination rites incorporate gestures of touch, especially the laying on of hands. A lesser distinction is made between the origin and the destination community when communion (a food rite) or profession (a verbal rite) is designated for the transition; a greater distinction is made when ecclesial transition is accomplished by handlaying or anointing, let alone baptism.

Considering the social body, rather than the theological distinction between penance and initiation, helps explain some of the complexities of the reception of the irregularly baptized throughout the centuries. We can distinguish two types of rites for belonging to a social body. One type concerns the essence or internal belonging of a member, and the other concerns the outer boundaries of that member. We would propose that in addition to communion, which symbolizes essential belonging through consumption, oral and

23. On the completeness of baptism among the churches of the Reformation, even those who maintain confirmation practice, see Colin O. Buchanan, *Baptism as Complete Sacramental Initiation*, Grove Worship Series 219 (Cambridge, England: Grove Books Limited, 2014).

written professions of faith signify essential belonging through the heart and words (Rom 10:9-10). Baptism, handlaying, and anointing are applied to the skin, highlighting the outside of the physical body. These practices, to different degrees depending on the act and its historical context, symbolize the outer boundary of the social body. Sanctifying the outside of the body before it participates in the essential rites of communion promotes a community's sense of internal solidarity and external security, distinguishing it from others in the surrounding world.

In some cases, reception affects the boundaries of the social body in a very literal way. Communal or ecclesial reception bears a more obviously ecumenical character, not only manifesting the boundaries of the church communion, but also changing them. Sometimes communion is reestablished between churches, for example by the resumption of the commemoration of the patriarchs and other hierarchs in the eucharistic prayer, which is a common mode for breaking and reestablishing communion in the East. Perhaps one of the most studied examples in the West outside of the patristic period is the bull *Exsultate Deo*, published by the Council of Florence in 1439, concerning the unification of the Armenian Church with Rome.

Also known as the "Decree for the Armenians," this document laid the groundwork for an eventual reconciliation between the Armenian Church and Rome. This reconciliation would likely include formal agreements, documentary and perhaps ritual, by Roman and Armenian ecclesial authorities, with no rites required of the individual priests and laity. This top-down approach has its sociological limits, as Douglas would suggest. For this reason, the reconciliation of East and West at the Council of Florence was a failure:

> The Council of Florence should serve as a warning. Both Romans and Byzantines had the misconception that the reunion of the two churches could be accomplished by an agreement between the leaders of the two churches. They failed to realize that the existential reunion of two such complex social bodies with their unique sensitivities could never be accomplished by a theoretical agreement through their representatives; not even if the representatives are in the highest positions in the respective hierarchies.[24]

At a smaller level, whole communities are generally received or reconciled using a rite drawn from the history of the group being received. The Anglican Ordinariate serves as an example: the process of establishing norms for those coming into full communion with Rome from the Anglican Communion was first authorized in 1980. But while John Paul II's "Pastoral Provision" for the United States allowed people coming into communion with the Catholic Church from the Anglican tradition to continue to use Anglican liturgical forms, such permissions were restricted to an individual basis. Benedict XVI's *Anglicanorum Coetibus* (2009), on the other hand, established ordinariates through a more communal and institutional

---

24. Ladislas M. Orsy, "Authentic Learning and Receiving—A Search for Criteria," in *Receptive Ecumenism and the Call to Catholic Learning: Exploring a Way for Contemporary Ecumenism*, ed. P. D. Murray and Luca Badini Confalonieri (Oxford/New York: Oxford University Press, 2010), 45.

process, adapting the rite of reception (albeit as a communal service) for communities being received into the Catholic Church.[25] Eventually, a specific rite was developed and included in *Divine Worship: Occasional Services*,[26] an official service book of the Anglican Ordinariates in communion with Rome. Clergy had to undergo the rite of reception before reordination to the diaconate and presbyterate under a formal and extended formation program. Even when not part of a whole community being received, there is generally a distinctive ritual process for those who are ordained and who will minister in their new communion as well. The reception of an ordained person is a different alteration of ecclesial boundaries than is the reception of the individual layperson.

In the Eastern Orthodox churches today, clergy of other churches may be received in a variety of ways. Most former Protestant clergy will be received by chrismation and reordination. Former Roman Catholics might be received by chrismation and "vesting," where

---

25. See James Matthew Sheehan, "A New Canonical Configuration for the 'Pastoral Provision' for Former Episcopalians in the United States of America?" (JCD diss., Pontifical University of the Holy Cross, 2009); Stephen Cavanaugh, *Anglicans and the Roman Catholic Church: Reflections on Recent Developments* (San Francisco: Ignatius Press, 2011); John Huels, "Canonical Comments on *Anglicanorum Coetibus*," *Worship* 84, no. 3 (2010): 237–53; James Daniel Bradley, "The Provenance and Purpose of Personal Ordinariates: Erected under the Auspices of the Apostolic Constitution *Anglicanorum Cætibus*" (JCD diss., The Catholic University of America, 2017). We are grateful to Bradley for his personal correspondence and assistance.

26. *Divine Worship: Occasional Services* (London: The Catholic Truth Society, 2014), 41–47.

the clergyman is clothed with Orthodox liturgical vestments and then concelebrates the Divine Liturgy with his new bishop. Roman Catholics may also, like Oriental Orthodox, be received by vesting alone to celebrate the Eucharist. Finally, some clergy will be received by rebaptism and reordination, depending on the jurisdiction receiving them. A series of ancient canons originally composed to govern particular situations—such as those from the fourth-century Novatian crisis or the ninth-century Iconoclastic dispute—might be invoked to justify such decisions.

More frequently, theological arguments are made which take into consideration the status of "apostolic succession" in the convert's church of origin or the existence of the "sacrament of holy orders" in that church, to take but two examples; also in play are the continuing debates over the existence of grace outside of the canonical boundaries of the Orthodox Church.[27] Peter Gillquist, a former Evangelical Protestant pastor, led more than a dozen church communities and several thousand congregants into the Antiochian Orthodox Church en masse in 1987. In smaller, albeit still communal, ceremonies, all of these converts were received by anointing with chrism, and those who were church pastors were chrismated and then ordained as Eastern Orthodox priests.[28] While the reception methods utilized here—chrismation and subsequent ordination—were

27. John H. Erickson, "Reception of Non-Orthodox Clergy into the Orthodox Church," *St. Vladimir's Theological Quarterly* 29 (1985): 115–32.

28. Peter E. Gillquist, *Becoming Orthodox: A Journey to the Ancient Christian Faith* (Brentwood, TN: Wolgemuth and Hyatt, 1989).

an adaptation of the typical approach to individual conversion, the scale and communal aspect are unique. Gillquist's group had first petitioned the Ecumenical Patriarch in Constantinople for similar treatment: what one Orthodox patriarchate (Constantinople) demurred from doing, another (Antioch) later welcomed.

The contemporary Roman Catholic Church has put its ecumenical energies into formal bilateral conversations with other Christian communions and discussions of what visible unity would mean, rather than continuing an earlier approach which saw Christian unity as a process to be accomplished by individual and group conversions.[29] This is in large part because the unity accomplished by these mass receptions is often counterbalanced by increased tensions between the churches of origin and the receiving group.[30] We will see this same dynamic reflected in the historical material as well.

As the ecumenical guidelines of the Catholic Church, the *Directory for the Application of Principles and Norms on Ecumenism* suggests that reception of baptized Christians and ecumenical efforts are interrelated but also in tension with one another.[31] Although on a

29. Harding Meyer, "Unity in Reconciled Diversity," in *The Oxford Handbook of Ecumenical Studies*, ed. Geoffrey Wainwright and Paul McPartlan (Oxford: Oxford University Press, 2021), 558–74.

30. On uniatism and Orthodoxy, see *Stolen Churches or Bridges to Orthodoxy?*, ed. Vladimir Latinovic and Anastasia K. Wooden, vol. 1, *Historical and Theological Perspectives on the Orthodox and Eastern Catholic Dialogue*, Pathways for Ecumenical and Interreligious Dialogue (Cham, Switzerland: Palgrave Macmillan, 2021).

31. The current (1993) Roman Catholic *Directory for the Application of Principles and Norms on Ecumenism* distinguishes the reception of baptized Christians from the ecumenical work of the

lesser scale, this is true of the reception of individuals as well as of clergy and larger groups. Rites of reception play a role in expressing and developing the church's understanding of the extent of the Christian body; at the same time, theological convictions can often be trumped in practice by sociological impulses.

------

church: "Every Christian has the right for conscientious religious reasons, freely to decide to come into full Catholic communion. The work of preparing the reception of an individual who wishes to be received into full communion with the Catholic Church is of its nature distinct from ecumenical activity." The document goes on to recommend, nonetheless, that pastors receiving Christians into the Roman Catholic Church must consult the proper ecumenical agreements to decide on the proper steps for their incorporation. Pontifical Council for Promoting Christian Unity, *Directory for the Application of Principles and Norms on Ecumenism* (Vatican City: Libreria Editrice Vaticana, 1993), §99; quoting without attribution from UR 4, which continues, "there is no opposition between the two, since both proceed from the marvelous ways of God."

Chapter Two

# The Historical Foundations

## Foundational Dispute: Cyprian and Stephen

The third-century debate over whether serious sinners and those baptized in other communities should be rebaptized has had a profound influence on initiation and ecumenical relationships, as well as on reception practices.[1] The debate originated with the problem of whether and how to readmit repentant apostates, but revealed larger ecclesiological questions. Did serious sin, schism, or heresy put one outside the bounds of the church? Was the Holy Spirit active outside the visible bounds of the church? Did the gestures of initiation need to be the same in different churches?

There were discussions about how to understand baptisms performed outside of the church in

---

1. This contention is ubiquitous in the literature. See, for example, the following and their bibliographies: Dale Sieverding, *The Reception of Baptized Christians: A History and Evaluation* (Chicago: Liturgy Training Publications, 2001), 1–11; Paul Turner, *When Other Christians Become Catholic* (Collegeville, MN: Liturgical Press, 2007), 20–23; John Klentos, "Rebaptizing Converts into the Orthodox Church: Old Perspectives on a New Problem," *Studia Liturgica* 29 (1999): 217–20.

ecclesiastical writings from Rome, Gaul, Alexandria, and North Africa.[2] There were also decisions from church councils in Cappadocia (ca. 230s) and in Anatolia before the middle of the third century.[3] The earliest tradition in both North Africa and Rome was to admit heretics, schismatics, and apostates through the imposition of hands, but a North African synod at Carthage

2. For instance, see Irenaeus of Lyons, *Démonstration de la Prédication Apostolique* 1.7, ed. Adelin Rousseau, SC 406 (Paris: Cerf, 1995), 244; Irenaeus of Lyons, *Contre Les Hérésies*, 1.21.1-4, ed. Adelin Rousseau and Louis Doutreleau, SC 264 (Paris: Cerf, 1979), 294–304; Clement of Alexandria, *Stromata* 1.19.96.1-2, ed. Marcel Caster, SC 30bis (Paris: Cerf, 2006), 121; Tertullian, *De praescriptione haereticorum* 29.2-3, ed. R.F. Refoulé, CCSL 1 (Turnhout: Brepols, 1954), 209; Tertullian, *De baptismo* 15.2, ed. E. Dekkers, CCSL 1 (Turnhout: Brepols, 1954), 290; Hippolytus, *Refutatio omnium haeresium* 9.12.25-26, ed. Paul Wendland, GCS 26 (Leipzig: J.C. Hinrichs, 1916), 250–51; Origen, *In Evangelium Iohannis* 6.33.165-168, 10.42.220, 10.43.298, ed. Cécile Blanc, SC 157 (Paris: Cerf, 1970), 256–66, 298.

3. For the council in Iconium (Cappadocia) in the 230s, see Firmilian of Caesarea, *Ep.* 75.7.4-5, ed. G. F. Diercks, CCSL 3C (Turnhout: Brepols, 1996), 588–89; for the council in Carthage around 235, convoked by the bishop Agrippinus, see Cyprian of Carthage, *Ep.* 71.3.2-71.4.1, ed. G. F. Diercks, CCSL 3C (Turnhout: Brepols, 1996), 521, and Cyprian, *Ep.* 73.3.1, ed. G. F. Diercks (Turnhout: Brepols, 1996), 532; for the council in Synnada (Anatolia) sometime before the 250s, see Dionysius of Alexandria, *Epistula 3*, reproduced in Eusebius, *Historia Ecclesiastica* 7.7.5, ed. Eduard Schwarz, Theodor Mommsen, and Friedhelm Winkelmann, GCS 6/2 (Berlin: Akademie Verlag, 1999 reprint of 1908 edition), 644. For a discussion of these councils, see J. Patout Burns, "On Rebaptism: Social Organization in the Third Century Church," *Journal of Early Christian Studies* 1, no. 4 (Winter 1993): 377; Everett Ferguson, *Baptism in the Early Church: History, Theology, and Liturgy in the First Five Centuries* (Grand Rapids, MI: Eerdmans, 2009), 380–81 and 395.

under Agrippinus authorized rebaptism instead.[4] This recent, local "tradition" was used by Cyprian to argue that baptisms by groups outside of the church were invalid.[5] On the one hand, as Will Cohen has argued, Cyprian's motive may have been "largely preventative," as he tried to restrict Christians from separating from the churches which possessed "legitimately consecrated bishops in apostolic succession."[6] On the other hand, as Patout Burns has shown, the divergence from the earlier practice held in common with Rome was largely due to each church's experience of the persecution, and by extension to their differing approaches to repentance among the apostates.[7]

The Roman and Carthaginian churches were impacted by the persecutions, but to very different degrees and in different ways. In Carthage, on the one hand, disputes over how to reconcile those who had apostatized under persecution caused the church to split into three different camps.[8] The "rigorists" believed that

---

4. Agrippinus was one of Cyprian's predecessors as bishop of Carthage. The exact date of this synod is not known, though some sources date it to 220. Burns, "On Rebaptism," 377; Maxwell E. Johnson, *The Rites of Christian Initiation: Their Evolution and Interpretation*, rev. exp. ed. (Collegeville, MN: Liturgical Press, 2007), 95.

5. Cyprian, *Ep.* 73.3.1, ed. Diercks (1996), 532. This position was rooted in their understanding of the relationship between God and the church; see Johnson, *Rites of Christian Initiation*, 94; Ferguson, *Baptism in the Early Church*, 388–92.

6. Will Cohen, "Sacraments and the Visible Unity of the Church," *Ecclesiology* 4, no. 1 (2007): 70.

7. See Burns, "On Rebaptism," *passim*.

8. Burns, "On Rebaptism," 375.

apostates could not be reconciled to the church at all. The "laxists" believed apostates could return without a formal process of reconciliation, and accepted "letters of peace" from the confessors who had suffered because of their faith.[9] Cyprian was trying to chart a moderating position between rigorists and laxists, but saw immediate reconciliation by letters as a threat to the bishop's authority and an unacceptable compromise of the holiness expected of the church. Moreover, "because the church of Christ is one and indivisible, only one of the three rival communities could be the true church and only that one possessed the Holy Spirit and the power to sanctify."[10] Facing a schism in the church in Carthage, Cyprian first followed the Roman practice and urged an extended practice of repentance, culminating in the imposition of hands. However, the North African church had traditionally placed a higher authority on the letters of peace issued by confessors for the lapsed than the Roman church did. When laxist clergy and apostates refused to follow the formal policy of extended reconciliation, instead arguing that the confessors' letters of peace gave them immediate reconciliation and readmittance,[11] Cyprian "excommunicated the rebels. Thereafter, he regarded the renegade clergy and their supporters among the confessors, the faithful and the fallen, as a schismatic communion cast away from the true and faithful church."[12]

9. Burns, "On Rebaptism," 371–72 and 383–85.
10. Burns, "On Rebaptism," 379.
11. Burns, "On Rebaptism," 371–72 and 383–85.
12. Burns, "On Rebaptism," 373.

Further interference in Carthage came from the claims of the rigorist bishop Novatian, who practiced rebaptism of heretics and apostates. A disputed election in Rome between Cornelius (r. 251–253) and Novatian led the latter to set up a rival rigorist bishop and church in Carthage, rejecting any process for reconciling apostates.[13] Now there were two rival churches to Cyprian's in Carthage. Cyprian, worried about the impact of more persecutions and the success of the laxist position, moved to admit all of the lapsed who had done penance and had the Roman church follow suit as well.[14]

At the same time, because he was so committed to the indivisibility and unity of the church, Cyprian believed that the sacraments celebrated by the Novatians lacked the power to transmit divine grace. He wrote, "the Church alone possesses the life-giving water and she alone has the power to baptize and cleanse men. . . . For the Church is one; and being one, she cannot at the one and the same time be both inside and outside."[15] For Cyprian, anyone baptized outside of the church by these Novatians had to be baptized by the church in order to reenter her communion.

The situation in Rome was quite different. Cornelius was succeeded in a short time by Lucius and then Stephen (r. 254–257). The Roman Church had rigorist rivals in

13. Burns, "On Rebaptism," 374–75 and 394.

14. Burns, "On Rebaptism," 376, 385–86, and 391.

15. Cyprian, *Ep.* 69.3.1, ed. Diercks (1996), 473–74. The English is from *The Letters of St. Cyprian of Carthage*, trans. and ed. G. W. Clarke, vol. 4, *Letters 68–82*, Ancient Christian Writers 47 (Mahwah, NJ: Newman Press, 1989), 34.

the Novatians; the more laxist members followed a penitential discipline for readmittance. Stephen was thus able to take a more laxist position than Cyprian.[16] Like Cyprian, he reconciled the lapsed by penance—but he also reconciled repentant Novatians to the church by the same ritual gesture of penitence, not by the church's baptism as Cyprian did. Whereas Cyprian was fending off laxists and rigorists, Stephen only had to deal with the latter. Thus, Stephen "was fending off the assault against the power of the ritual of repentance to purify sinners and protect the church."[17]

At this time, there was a great deal of tolerance for variant practices in different local churches. The different approaches to receiving heretics of Rome and Carthage would likely have been tolerated by the broader church had Stephen not broken communion with Cyprian.[18] The dispute appears to have come to a head as a result of Stephen's support of a rigorist bishop in Arles as well as two lapsed bishops who sought to be reinstated to their offices in Spain. Cyprian disagreed with Stephen on maintaining communion with the former, and he was vehemently opposed to Stephen's support of the lapsed Spanish bishops' reinstatements rather than their laicization, as Cornelius had done with the lapsed bishop Trofimus.[19] As a result, Cyprian charged Stephen with breaking with custom and polluting the Roman Church by allowing lapsed clergy to retain their offices.[20] Stephen,

16. Burns, "On Rebaptism," 396.
17. Burns, "On Rebaptism," 397.
18. Burns, "On Rebaptism," 377–78 and 379.
19. Burns, "On Rebaptism," 376.
20. Burns, "On Rebaptism," 377n64.

for his part, seems to have believed that the position of Cyprian and the other North African bishops—that an imposition of hands was not enough to reconcile heretics and schismatics—mirrored Novatian's rigorist arguments.[21] As Burns notes, Stephen "never perceived a threat to the purity or identity of his church; he never regarded schismatics at home or dissenters abroad as denizens of the demonic realm from which he must shield his church. Instead, he viewed them as rebels within the kingdom of Christ whom he must discipline and subject to his apostolic authority."[22] In addition to denying a local tradition of reconciling heretics by imposing hands,[23] the North African policy of rebaptism seems to have been overly rigorist for Stephen's taste.

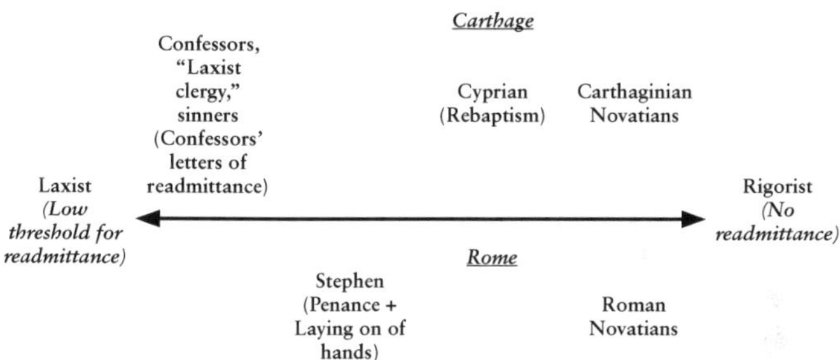


**Figure 2.1.** The spectrum of positions taken during the third-century debates about how to receive converts into the church. Above the axis are depicted groups operating in Carthage, while beneath the axis are depicted the conflicting parties in Rome. Preferred reception methods for some parties are included in parentheses.

21. Burns, "On Rebaptism," 399–400.
22. Burns, "On Rebaptism," 401.
23. According to Eusebius, *Historia Ecclesiastica* 7.3.3-4, ed. Schwarz, Mommsen, and Winkelmann (1999), 638.

It is ironic that Cyprian's position stemmed from an attempt to create a middle position between the laxists and rigorists in Carthage. Cyprian had argued that all those baptized as heretics seeking communion with the church should receive the full rites of initiation, which in Cyprian's time included rebaptism, the laying on of hands, and chrismation.[24] As he wrote to Stephen,

> [I]n the case of those who have been bathed beyond and outside the Church and have thus become stained and polluted by the unholy water of heretics and schismatics, when they come to us and the Church (which is one), they must be baptized. And the reason is that it is not sufficient just to lay hands upon them for receiving the Holy Spirit, unless they also receive a baptism of the Church. It is written: *Unless a man has been born of water and the Spirit, he cannot enter the kingdom of God.*[25]

In this letter, Epistle 72, Cyprian argues that a convert coming from outside the church, regardless of where he or she comes from, must receive the washing of bap-

24. Johnson, *Rites of Christian Initiation*, 84–95.

25. Cyprian, *Ep.* 72.1.1-2, ed. Diercks (1996), 523–24. "[E]os qui sint foris extra ecclesiam tincti et apud haereticos et schismaticos profanae aquae labe maculati, quando ad nos atque ad ecclesiam quae una est uenerint, baptizari oportere, eo quod parum sit eis manum inponere ad accipiendum spiritum sanctum, nisi accipiant et ecclesiae baptismum. Tunc enim demum plene sanctificari et esse filii dei possunt, si sacramento utroque nascantur, cum scriptum sit: *nisi quis natus fuerit ex aqua et spiritu, non potest introire in regnum dei.*" The English is from Cyprian, *Letters*, ed. Clarke, 4:52.

tism as well as the post-immersion imposition of hands, distinguished here from the gesture of penitential reconciliation. In other words, he distinguished between the baptismal bath of regeneration and the post-immersion imposition which transmitted the Holy Spirit upon the baptizand. Elsewhere (Epistle 70),[26] Cyprian also mentions the lack of chrism among the heretics, additionally implying the necessity of an anointing with chrism during this "new" initiation—a known ritual gesture at the time in North African baptismal practices.[27] For Cyprian, the convert could enter the church only by means of the entire *cursus* of initiation. If a person had not yet been regenerated by water and given the gift of the Spirit by the church's imposition of hands, he or she was not yet a member of the church—and, therefore, was simply not capacitated to be reconciled to the church by penance.

Apostates, on the other hand, were Christians who had been baptized in the church but who also had been alienated from that body by denying Christ during persecutions or by drifting into heresy. They could thus be reconciled merely with the laying on of hands as in penance. Both Cyprian and Stephen agreed on this latter point. But Stephen seems to have seen baptism of heretics and schismatics outside the church as valid. Perhaps he considered heresy and apostasy to be similar, but since his writings were not preserved,

26. Cyprian, *Ep.* 70.2.2, ed. Diercks (1996), 507.

27. See Johnson, *Rites of Christian Initiation*, 84–85, 90; Daniel Stramara, "Toward a Chrismatic Ecclesiology as a Theological Basis for Primacy," *Journal of Ecumenical Studies* 49, no. 2 (2014): 222.

we are dependent on his correspondents.[28] Writing to a colleague in his Epistle 74, Cyprian purports to quote from Stephen's own words, but first provides his own opinion on Stephen's position: " 'And so, in the case of those who may come to you from any heresy whatsoever, let there be no innovation beyond what has been handed down: hands are to be laid on them in penitence, since amongst heretics themselves they do not use their own rite of baptism on other heretics when they come to them, but they simply admit them to communion.' "[29] At least according to his rival, Cyprian, Stephen believed that everyone coming from outside of the church, regardless of their community of origin, should be received in the same way. That is, he believed that apostates, heretics, and schismatics should all be admitted into the church through the laying on of hands as in reconciliation.

Some of the confusion stemmed from the use of the same ritual gesture—handlaying—in both the rites of initiation and reconciliation. Cyprian may have believed that Stephen (or some of his followers) thought schismatics' baptism was effective but that the Holy Spirit is not given in the laying on of hands at baptism by schismatics. This made little sense to Cyprian:

28. Cyprian's Epistle 68 and Epistle 72 both purport to quote and summarize Stephen's arguments, as does Firmilian's Epistle 75. For the texts of these letters, see Cyprian, *Epistularium. Epistulae 58–81*, ed. G. F. Diercks, CCSL 3C (Turnhout: Brepols, 1996).

29. Cyprian, *Ep.* 74.1.2, ed. Diercks (1996), 564. English translation from Cyprian, *Letters*, ed. Clarke, 4:70.

> Cyprian detects an inconsistency in attributing power to the name of Christ in baptism that is not acknowledged in the case of the postbaptismal imposition of hands. However, the inconsistency exists only in Cyprian's understanding of the two ceremonies. For Stephen the laying on of hands when the heretic joined the catholic church was the same action used in reconciling penitents. . . . This could have been considered a renewing of the Holy Spirit, but it had nothing to do with whether a person had received the Holy Spirit in connection with baptism.[30]

Cyprian seems to have thought that Stephen was performing the post-baptismal imposition of hands, not a penitential imposition of hands. Unfortunately, Stephen's position is not entirely clear. As Burns notes, "[i]f Stephen did specify more fully the effects of the baptismal ritual and the mode of the Holy Spirit's operation in a schismatic community, these clarifications have escaped the historical record."[31] Nevertheless, Stephen's understanding appears to be rooted in a less direct identification between God's working in the world and the visible church,[32] and leaves a lot of uncertainty about the role of the Holy Spirit in schismatic communities and in the baptism proper.[33]

Stephen and Cyprian are the start of a long line of thinkers who will come to see the reception of heretics, schismatics, and apostates as either a completion of the

---

30. Ferguson, *Baptism in the Early Church*, 384.

31. Burns, "On Rebaptism," 398–99. See also 391–92.

32. Burns, "On Rebaptism," 387 and 397–98.

33. Burns, "On Rebaptism," 398–99; Ferguson, *Baptism in the Early Church*, 384, 392, 395, and 396–98.

process of initiation or as an act of reconciliation. For Cyprian the reception of apostates was an act of reconciliation, and the reception of heretics was a process of initiation. For Stephen both were rooted in a rite of reconciliation.[34] But in the early period, this distinction was not very clear: after all, baptism itself was a repentance and renunciation of sin. In fact, Burns notes that "the dispute could be characterized as a conflict over the rights and privileges of penitents as a class of persons within the church."[35] In other words, this was fundamentally a dispute about penance and its relation to initiation. This is clear in Stephen's approach, but can also be seen in Cyprian's writings. Initially, as noted above, Cyprian first followed the Roman practice for those who had lapsed, urging an extended practice of repentance culminating in the imposition of hands. However, when the period of extended practice of repentance was not followed, and individuals sought to short-circuit this process through the letters of confessors, Cyprian shifted his approach and made the matter more about initiation. The result was that Cyprian's church in Carthage had less "confidence in the efficacy or efficiency of the ritual of reconciliation" than the church in Rome did.[36]

34. John H. Erickson, "Divergences in Pastoral Practice in the Reception of Converts," in *Orthodox Perspectives on Pastoral Praxis: Papers of Intra-Orthodox Conference on Pastoral Praxis (24-25 September 1986) Celebrating the 50th Anniversary of Holy Cross Greek Orthodox School of Theology (1937-1987)*, ed. Theodore Stylianopoulos (Brookline, MA: Holy Cross Orthodox Press, 1988), 154.

35. Burns, "On Rebaptism," 387.

36. Burns, "On Rebaptism," 384.

Cyprian and Stephen's dispute became a topic of widespread Christian controversy. Cyprian was able to marshal widespread support for his position across the Christian world. Firmilian of Caesarea would side with Cyprian against Stephen, while Dionysius of Alexandria seems to have vacillated between Cyprian and Stephen's positions, but was strongly opposed (like Cyprian) to Stephen breaking communion with churches over the issue. Other writers in this period were advocating for a moderating position between the positions of Cyprian and Stephen.[37] An example of a moderating position comes from the anonymous tract *On Rebaptism*, likely written by a North African opponent of Cyprian.[38] The tract lumps heretics and schismatics into the same category and attributes the power of baptism not to the minister or the church but to the invocation of the name of Christ, a position which seems close to Stephen's. As a result, the writer argues that some baptisms celebrated outside of the

37. For a more detailed discussion of this period, see Burns, "On Rebaptism," 378, 384; and Ferguson, *Baptism in the Early Church*, 385–88, 394–98.

38. On this document, *De rebaptismate*, see Laurence Decousu, *Le perte de l'Esprit Saint et son recouvrement dans L'Église ancienne: La réconciliation des hérétiques et des penitents en Occident du III^e siècle jusqu'à Grégoire le Grand*, Brill's Studies in Catholic Theology 1 (Leiden: Brill, 2015), 23–27; for a textual history, see Paul Mattei, "*Remarques sue la tradition (manuscrite et imprimée) du* De rebaptismate," in *Critica Philologica, Nachleben, First Two Centuries, Tertullian and Arnobius, Egypt before Nicaea, Athanasius and his Opponents*, ed. M. F. Wiles and E. J. Yarnold, Studia Patristica 36 (Leuven: Peeters, 2001), 35–45. For a summary of the document, see Ferguson, 385–88.

church can be acknowledged as valid. If they have received such a baptism, those who desire to enter the church from outside groups simply need to receive the imposition of hands for the reception of the Holy Spirit. As a result, the writer distinguishes between the baptism itself and the bestowal of the Holy Spirit:

> If, however, it was conferred by those unknown to us, let the matter be corrected as is possible and is permitted. Since there is no Holy Spirit outside the Church, there can be no sound faith not only among the heretics but also among those in schism. Therefore those who do penance and are reformed through the teaching of truth and through their own faith, a faith that has later been improved by a purified heart, should be aided only by a spiritual baptism, that is, by the imposition of the bishop's hand and by the supplying of the Holy Spirit.[39]

As Ferguson notes, "[t]he imposition of hands on those formerly baptized in a group outside the communion of the church thus served both to complete their baptism and to reconcile them to the church."[40] The writer of *On Rebaptism* sees this imposition of hands not as simply a matter of reconciliation but also a completion of initiation. It is also important to rec-

39. *De rebaptismate* 10, in *S. Thasci Caecili Cypriani Opera Omnia*, vol. 3, ed. William Hartel, CSEL 3/3 (Vienna: Geroldi, 1871), 82. The English is from *Worship in the Early Church: An Anthology of Sources*, vol. 1, ed. Lawrence J. Johnson (Collegeville, MN: Liturgical Press, 2009), 190.

40. Ferguson, *Baptism in the Early Church*, 386.

ognize that the anonymous writer did acknowledge that some baptisms were unacceptable to the church. Converts would require a "repeated baptism" (*baptisma iteratum*), a "second and perfected seal of the faith," if their baptisms outside the church had not been celebrated "in the name of Jesus Christ."[41] Despite Cyprian's complaint that Stephen indiscriminately accepted all converts by the imposition of hands, it is difficult to determine from the limited evidence the extent to which the nuanced position of *On Rebaptism* may have differed from Stephen's position.

Already in the Latin-speaking world of the third century, if not before, the water bath and other gestures (anointing and the laying on of hands) were considered to be theologically and ritually separable from one another. Even if they usually did coincide in the one rite of baptism, it was possible to deploy them separately to deal with ritual issues in the original baptism. Likewise, there were already disputes in Latin theology over which (or whether both) bestowed the Holy Spirit. This would be further affirmed in the manner for receiving heretics in the First Council of Arles (can. 9 [8]), the Council of Elvira, and ultimately the Council of Nicaea.

41. "The question is whether, conforming to the most ancient practice and ecclesiastical tradition, it suffices that since they were baptized outside the Church but in the name of Jesus Christ our Lord only the hand of the bishop be imposed on them for receiving the Holy Spirit, this imposition giving them a second and perfected seal of the faith. Or must they be baptized again since, lacking this, they receive nothing just as if they had never been baptized in the name of Jesus Christ?" *De rebaptismate* 1, ed. Hartel, CSEL 3/3, 69–70. The English is from *Worship in the Early Church*, ed. Johnson, 1:185–86.

These debates played a role in setting the stage for the gradual emergence of "confirmation" in the West.[42]

The key moderating position in the debate—the anonymous tract *On Rebaptism*—serves as a forerunner in many ways to Augustine's later theology of the sacraments. The Augustinian position acknowledged the existence of baptisms outside of the church which are valid but which need to be enlivened by the church with the charity of the Holy Spirit through the imposition of hands. While there is no evidence that the anonymous Latin treatise influenced the Eastern approach to receiving converts, one can nonetheless find parallels with later Greek tradition in *On Rebaptism*. Much like the Byzantine liturgists and theologians of later centuries, the writer of this North African treatise understood the liturgical reception of a heretic as the final step of initiation, while referring to the ritual gesture by which they were received as a kind of corrective measure in a vaguely improper baptism.[43]

## Mary Douglas and Cultural Theory

Why would handlaying and chrismation emerge in both penance and initiation and become a source of confusion? How can cultural theory give us a new perspective on the debate over handlaying in third-century Rome and Carthage? In her earlier and better-known works, Douglas treats the social constitution of groups

42. For a summary, see Johnson, *Rites of Christian Initiation*, 247–59.

43. See, e.g., *Quaestiones et responsiones ad Orthodoxos* 14, PG 6:1249–1400, and the discussion on p. 58 below.

by their "group" and "grid," as if they are in isolation from other groups. In her late works, she thinks instead about the way complex societies are composed of different factions, each of which has a culture of its own and lives by relationship with other factions. The complex society, called the city, contains different communities who are organized differently. The core or central community maintains a set of robust and nuanced categories by means of hierarchy, bureaucracy, and generally accepted legislative and intellectual power. The accepted and nuanced distinctions, called high "grid," are not merely power differentials, but also include different ways of knowing and concepts of belonging. The central community also tends to be composed of "institutional thinkers" who hold the good of the community (here, their ecclesial community) as more important than their own self-interest. This leads to a strong sense of collective solidarity, which she calls high "group." In figure 2.2, "group" is on the horizontal axis and "grid" on the vertical axis. The bureaucratic center has a high value for both.

Other groups (sectarian or dissenting enclaves) that are part of the complex society maintain their identity by rejecting the categories ("grid") of the bureaucracy, while maintaining strong outer boundaries and inner solidarity (high "group"; that is, the lower right of figure 2.2). These communities often feel their identity to be under threat from the bureaucracy or from outside agents. Perhaps they have been marginalized by the central community or are purposely seceding from it. Perhaps they are simply far away from the central community and ensconced in a different kind of power struggle. These communities may have char-

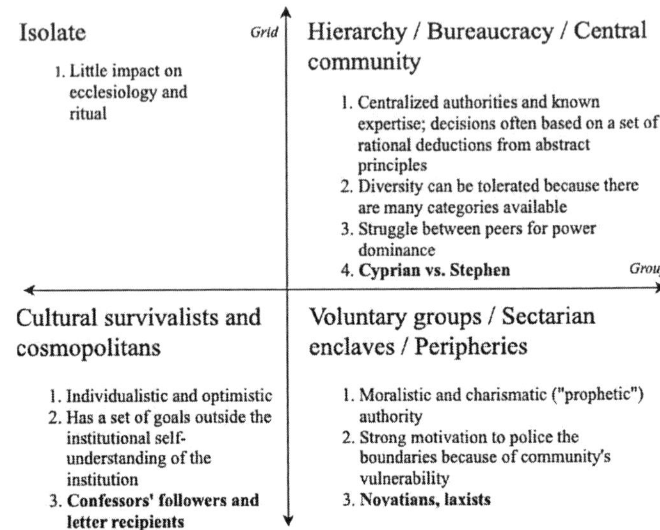


**Figure 2.2.** Representatives of each type of cultural community from the North African and Roman debate over rebaptism. Each axis represents a spectrum that might vary among representatives. Regular text summarizes the characteristics of each type of cultural community; bold text provides specific examples from this historical period.

ismatic leadership, but their membership tends to be more egalitarian. Ritual practices initiating members that come from the dominant community (if this is even possible) will be especially important and likely elaborate, but there may also be an emphasis on the *communitas*[44] or solidarity of the community itself.

44. The word comes from Victor Turner, *The Ritual Process: Structure and Anti-Structure* (Chicago: Aldine, 1969).

> Dissenting minorities are always present in the
> city, though often unrecognized or refused the
> recognition they demand. They do not have in-
> ternally structured complementary and counter-
> vailing sections, nor do they organize by ranked,
> separate compartments. Christian Church history
> gives many examples of the non-conformist reli-
> gions. . . . Their cultural attitudes are coloured
> by their ongoing protest against the centre com-
> munity which has pushed them into an enclave by
> rejecting their principles.[45]

By requiring equal purity of all members and performing the most intense skin rite on those coming from
outside the community, the Novatian rigorists in Carthage became a dissenting enclave: they exhibited high
barriers to entry and resistance to the hierarchical authority of the bishop.

A central community usually has an internal tension
between two main factions, and members of the central
community tend to misinterpret outside communities as
if they are governed by the same polarizing questions
that construct these factions. Rites within this central
community create "grid," showcasing the internal structures or orderings that make complex categories intellectually and juridically manageable. They move people
and things from one internal category to another. They
are also used to enforce internal relationships: it is in
the rites of the central community that laying a hand
on someone's head, for instance, signifies authority and

45. Mary Douglas, "The Self as Risk-Taker: A Cultural Theory
of Contagion in Relation to AIDS," in *Risk and Blame: Essays in
Cultural Theory* (New York: Routledge, 2003), 105.

power over them. The dispute between Carthage and Rome over the reconciliation of heretics and apostates is an argument about the categories where "apostate" and "Novatian" fit and the proper rites necessary to receive them back into the church. Cyprian felt that these two distinct categories should be received by different means: the first by imposition of hands and the second by a valid initiation rite. Stephen believed they should both be received by imposition of hands.

On the other hand, both the rigorists and the laxists who set up their own communities denied the necessity of the hierarchical rite of reconciliation: the imposition of the bishop's hand on the head of the apostate. These dissenting enclaves were primarily defined by the ways each rejected the central community's "grid."

Although enclaves and bureaucracies have opposing ways of knowing and identifying themselves, and tensions emerge from that opposition, each have relatively clear outer boundaries from their own perspective and value being able to differentiate groups from one another. Cultural survivalists[46] or cosmopolitans, on the other hand, primarily act as individual agents that may traverse the boundaries between groups to achieve their own political goals. Again, high-group communities, whether enclaves or hierarchies, may see cultural survivalists as part of one or another group, but they themselves are likely to make use of each system as need be. One should not accuse them of being reckless or cavalier, since the motivation may be survival or liberation as easily as personal power or

---

46. Douglas's term is "cultural frontiersmen," which we have adjusted for gender neutrality, attempting to preserve some of its semantic field.

gain. Unlike members of enclaves or hierarchies, they do not see their own interests as being identifiable with any of the institutions on offer, though they make use of the forms of one or another group. In the historical narratives we will be exploring, the cultural survivalists are generally local political leaders, whose ecclesial belonging tends to be in the service of political stability for their nation and their own rule.

There have likely been isolates in the Christian churches all along, too—members who see themselves as totally unable to affect the progress of history, who speak for no group and see none as speaking for them. Douglas does not examine this group closely, and they also do not create much liturgical documentation or ecclesial movement, so we will not be exploring their views further.

Most of our documentary evidence in liturgical history reflects the perspective of those legislating usage (i.e., the central community). In the reception of baptized Christians, we will see that each of these institutions has, until the mid-twentieth century if not to the present day, been mostly concerned with how practices of reception positively or negatively impact their relationships with one another and with other relatively centralized institutional churches. Communities on the margins between East and West or under other extreme stressors, on the other hand, may tend to elaborate rites for reception out of a concern for the community's boundaries. Ecumenical relations have sometimes suffered when a church pits their own community's centralized tolerance against another group's dissident practices of intolerance. Understanding the sociological pressures influencing local communities, in those cases, can help us be more honest.

Baptizing Christians who have been baptized in other communities communicates a rejection of those communities' legitimacy as parts of the universal Christian church. This was the position of the Novatians. The ritual gestures of handlaying and anointing, on the other hand, permitted a variety of interpretations, and this was, in fact, part of the issue between Cyprian and Stephen. The use of the same ritual gesture, namely the laying on of hands, in different ritual contexts caused some confusion but also enabled some flexibility. Today, ambiguity about the function of these different ritual gestures allows some of the churches to remain agnostic about the permeability of the boundaries of the social body of Christ's church.

Both chrismation and handlaying rites include touching the candidate's head with the hand of an authority from the new ecclesial communion. Because an individual's body represents the social body, the hand signifies power and authority (after all, it is primarily the hands by which people influence the world around them) and the head signifies the whole body. When a bishop lays a hand on the head of a person to be received, therefore, at an anthropological level this gesture demonstrates the bishop's complete authority over the person being received. The use of chrism, too, creates a physical connection between the head of a particular church and the body of the person being initiated. Between handlaying and chrismation, the scent of chrism makes the gesture more symbolically intense and lasting. The two are symbolically cognate[47]—especially if the bishop is

---

47. Nathan Chase, "Anointings with Oil and Handlaying in the Early Church: Early Ritual Cognates?" Presented at the conference on "Öl in der frühen Liturgie: Verwendung und Deutung," Regensburg, February 9, 2024.

present—but represent a spectrum of intensity, where more intensity might be necessary to overcome a steeper boundary of the social body. For Stephen, these rites left room for the recognition of a candidate's initiation but also retained the sociological security of a high-group community. However, Cyprian and the rigorists rejected this interpretation since it was necessary for all of the initiatory rituals to be performed by a legitimate bishop. For Cyprian, this was a way to maintain control, particularly in distinction to the laxists' community, and to reinforce his own position vis-à-vis the rigorists. For Stephen, who had less steep boundaries for the social body because his community was less insecure, a less intense ritual gesture—the laying on of hands—was all that was needed, though this still allowed for control of the social body.

Communities that receive new members with only a verbal profession or written letter, on the other hand, have lower outer boundaries than the high-group communities on the right side of Fig. 2.2. Communities with low-group characteristics tend to have less internal bonding and their members act more as cultural survivalists. This is consistent with the behavior of those seeking letters from the confessors in Carthage.

Obviously, these sociological factors are not by any means the only factors influencing Christian history. In fact, in the ecumenical movement there is a concerted effort to reject psychological security measures to be more faithful to our theological ideals about the scope of Christ's church, and there have certainly been other instances of this in ecclesial history. But when there is an ongoing conflict between theological concepts and ritual practice, the sociological principles can help us understand the draw of a theologically inapposite symbolism.

The debate between Cyprian and Stephen represents the first major clash on the ritual and theology associated with the reception of apostates and heretics into the church.[48] In their debate, they set the parameters for how the reception of baptized Christians would be treated up to the present day. While Maxwell Johnson contends that "history shows that it was the view of Stephen and the Church of Rome that ultimately triumphed in this controversy," this is an oversimplification.[49] Doctrinally, the fourth to eighth centuries would ensure the triumph of the principle that trinitarian baptism outside the church should be accepted without rebaptism, but the practice—in both East and West—often diverged from this norm. The centuries of rebaptism of baptized converts in East and West, against the clear norms of their legislative authorities, have much to teach us about the challenges of receiving and implementing ecumenical norms in the churches today.

48. See Erickson, "Divergences," 153. Erickson in particular is helpful in showing that Cyprian was not the first to suggest rebaptism: "Though Cyprian was not the first or only churchman to insist that heretics must be (re)baptized, he certainly was one of the first to insist categorically on the (re)baptism of all those baptized 'outside.'"

49. Johnson, *Rites of Christian Initiation*, 95.

Chapter Three

# Clarifying the Debate

*From Cyprian and Stephen to the First
Liturgical Witnesses*

Both Cyprian and Stephen were using handlaying to manage local crises about how to understand baptism by separated communities and whether and how apostates and other serious sinners could be received into the church. Nonetheless, concepts established by their local and time-dependent debate eventually came to be seen as normative for global and enduring churches. Local synods, too, that originally were developed to deal with specific historical situations were gradually adopted over a broader geographical area as norms, to which later synods held local practices accountable. In the early church, each diocese or metropolitan area had its own primary dissenting groups, generally around christological or trinitarian theology, as well as apostates who repudiated the faith under persecution. In the West, reception was primarily made by the laying on of hands; in the East, it was done by chrismation and renunciations.

## Trinitarian Baptism in East and West

The Western Council of Arles (ca. 314) was a synod of the Latin-speaking dioceses convoked by the emperor Constantine. This gave it authority within the Western part of the church (who was represented at the council), but it was never received into Eastern canons.[1] The Council of Arles issued a canon ordering that no one baptized into the Trinity should be rebaptized upon entry to the church. They were to be received by imposition of hands for the reception of the Holy Spirit.[2]

The imposition of hands, which was to become the primary gesture of reception in the West, was not necessarily seen as a completion of initiation, nor was it a reconciliation after serious sin. Rather, the imposition of hands seems to have served multiple symbolic purposes. On one hand, the gesture of authority on the outer boundary of the initiate's body marked a clear threshold between the community they came from and the one they were received into. On the other hand, it was associated with the Holy Spirit, whose assistance was necessary for any transition.

Even though the Council of Arles was not received as authoritative in the East, the principle that trinitar-

1. For a discussion, see Francis J. Thomson, "Economy: An Examination of the Various Theories of Economy Held within the Orthodox Church, with Special Reference to the Ecumenical Recognition of the Validity of Non-Orthodox Sacraments," *Journal of Theological Studies*, New Series 16, no. 2 (October 1965): 403.

2. For the text of Arles can. 9 (8), see *Ecclesiae Occidentalis Monumenta Iuris Antiquissima: Canonum et Conciliorum Graecorum Interpretationes Latinae*, vol. 1, ed. Cuthbert Hamilton Turner (Oxford: Clarendon, 1913), 387–88.

ian baptism was the standard for belonging eventually came to be accepted in the East as well. The canons of the Council of Nicaea (325) clearly decreed that some baptisms "performed outside" of the church—to use Cyprian's language—were, in fact, acceptable to the church. The Novatians, a sect with a trinitarian creed but who refused to readmit apostates, were to be received by an imposition of hands (can. 8), while the lapsed were to be reconciled by penance (can. 11). The Paulianists, who baptized in the name of Father, Son, and Spirit but who were monarchianists—i.e., they professed a non-trinitarian interpretation of faith—needed to be rebaptized (can. 19).[3]

Boundary rites were not always reciprocal. The Novatians, for example, required catholics to be rebaptized on entering the sect, but the catholics received the Novatians by handlaying. (At this point, the term "Catholic Church" and "catholics" included both Eastern and Western trinitarian Christians, in communion with bishops of recognized apostolic succession.) The Donatists required that those received into their group be rebaptized, but the catholics received them without rebaptizing. In each place, the central community implemented its interpretation of ecclesiological principles about baptism. After Nicaea, in both Eastern and Western practice, this normative standard included

---

3. For a discussion of monarchian theology, see J. N. D. Kelly, *Early Christian Doctrines*, 4th ed. (London: Adam and Charles Black, 1968), 115–19. For the text of these canons of I Nicaea, see *Corpus Christianorum Conciliorum Oecumenicorum Generaliumque Decreta*, vol. 1, ed. Giuseppe Alberigo (Turnhout: Brepols, 2006–present), 24, 25–26, 30.

baptism in the name of the Trinity *and* trinitarian faith. As we will see in the next chapter, small, threatened communities on the margins—even those in communion with the central community—often ignore the official boundaries and canons because of their need for higher thresholds of entry.

The Eastern canonical tradition, instead of the single gesture of imposition of hands, gradually established an imaginary set of "concentric rings" of each tradition's nearness to orthodoxy. Depending on how far a heresy was from "orthodox" faith—this term, like "catholic," would have described both Eastern and Western trinitarian Christians at this period—a different set of rites of reception was called for. Groups that were judged to have an appropriate trinitarian theology were usually received by anathema (a verbal renunciation of previous heresy) and chrismation (anointing with chrism). This was a lower threshold. Groups who did not practice valid baptism or who did not have an adequate trinitarian theology were rebaptized, constituting a higher threshold. The Council of Laodicea (ca. 363/364), for instance, ordered catechism, anathema, and chrismation for converted Novatians, Photinians, and Quartodecimans (can. 7), and rebaptism of monarchian Montanists (can. 8).[4] Against the Eunomians, an anonymous Syrian council around 380 insisted on rebaptism for those *not* baptized into three immersions with a trinitarian invocation (= "Apostolic Canon" 50).[5]

---

4. For the text of Laodicea can. 7 and 8, see *Discipline générale antique (IV*e*–IX*e* s.)*, vol. 1/2, ed. Périclès-Pierre Joannou, Fonti 9 (Grottaferrata, Italy: Tipografia Italo-Orientale S. Nilo, 1962–1964), 133–34.

5. Importantly, "Apostolic Canon" 47 did not permit the rebaptism of those who had received "true baptism." For the text, see *Ap-*

These norms were intended only for the specific groups named. Responding theologically to actual situations in the church's life,[6] the canons prescribed concrete liturgical methods for the reception of converts from each of these active groups. This synodal approach—local and temporally limited—was important because there was significant variation among the followers of particular theological teachers throughout the Christian world at the time, as well as from generation to generation within a heretical movement. The "Montanists" of fourth-century Syria and the "Montanists" of fifth-century North Africa might not be the same. Therefore, the canons were evaluated for application to each new situation as it arose.

In succeeding years, Eastern theologians interpreted these categories in various ways. In the 370s, Basil the Great in his Epistle 188 (= Basil can. 1[7]) demanded the

---

*ostolic Constitutions* 8.47.47, ed. M. Metzger, *Les Constitutions Apostoliques*, SC 336 (Paris: Editions du Cerf, 1987), 3:290; for the text of Apostolic Canon 50, see *Apostolic Constitutions* 8.47.50, ed. Metzger (1987), 3:290, 292. For the fourth-century, anti-Eunomian origins of this ostensibly "apostolic" legislation, see David Heith-Stade, "Receiving the Non-Orthodox: A Historical Study of Greek Orthodox Canon Law," *Studia Canonica* 44, no. 2 (2010): 410.

6. For this interpretation of the canonical tradition's evolution, at least in the Byzantine East, see Vladimir Lossky, *The Mystical Theology of the Eastern Church* (Cambridge: James Clarke, 1957), 175; Nicholas N. Afanasiev, "The Canons of the Church: Changeable or Unchangeable?," *St. Vladimir's Theological Quarterly* 11, no. 2 (1967): 58.

7. Basil's canonical guidance to his disciple Amphilochius of Iconium eventually entered the Eastern canonical tradition in the sixth century when it was included in the canonical collections being developed to help guide ecclesiastical practice. See Heith-Stade, "Receiving the Non-Orthodox," 408.

rebaptism of all those who could be called "heretics," that is, those who were "completely broken off and estranged to the faith itself."[8] Using the example of Montanist non-trinitarian baptism, he argued that baptism should include the trinitarian invocation,[9] while those with an acceptably trinitarian faith and baptism, such as the Encratites, could be received by the anointing with chrism.[10] Finally, Didymus of Alexandria (ca. 313–398) provided one possible justification for the practice of chrismating heretics who returned to the church. In his *De trinitate*, he argued that chrismation was meant to complete initiation: heretical sects do not have valid bishops so their chrism was not valid, an essential part of the baptismal rites for Christians in the eastern part of the empire.[11] No equivalent concern about chrism was raised in the West before the Reformation.[12]

8. The English translation is from Basil of Caesarea, "*Canonical Letters* (Letters 188, 199, and 217)," in *The Cambridge Edition of Early Christian Writings*, vol. 2, *Practice*, ed. Ellen Muehlberger, trans. Andrew Radde-Gallwitz (Cambridge/New York: Cambridge University Press, 2017), 145; the Greek can be found in Saint Basil, *Lettres*, vol. 2, ed. Yves Courtonne (Paris: Société d'Édition Les Belles Lettres, 1961), 121.

9. Basil, *Epistula* 188, ed. Courtonne, 2:122.

10. Basil, *Epistula* 188, ed. Courtonne, 2:123–24.

11. Didymus of Alexandria, *De trinitate* 2.15, PG 39:720–21.

12. The conflict in the West in this period concerned priests who wished to consecrate the chrism, not heretical groups. See, for example, the Spanish councils: Nathan Chase, "From Arianism to Orthodoxy: The Role of the Rites of Initiation in Uniting the Visigothic Kingdom," *Hispania Sacra* 72:146 (2020): 427–38. After the Reformation, the issue of who can consecrate chrism and perform these rites appears again, given that chrism blessed in the churches of the Reformation is not always blessed by a bishop

Around the same time, in the Western part of the empire, there was some variance between handlaying and chrismation for the reception of Christians from heretical groups. Pope Siricius (r. 384–399) wrote to Himerius, bishop of Tarragona in Spain, and said that the Novatians should be reconciled "only through the sole invocation of the seven-fold Spirit by the imposition of a bishop's hand."[13] The letter suggests that some heretics in the West, like those in the East, were rebaptizing catholics who joined them, but the Western Church was imposing hands to receive those from these groups, acknowledging their previous baptism as valid.[14] Innocent I (r. 401–417) interpreted reception as simultaneously a renunciation and an infusion of the Holy Spirit, saying that hand laying was "under the symbol of penitence and sanctification of the Holy Spirit" (*Ep.* 24.4).[15] The Council of Orange (441),

----

and the validity—from the Roman perspective—of that bishop's ordination is in question. In a sense, the modern period has seen a rehashing of the older North African and Spanish debates again.

13. "[P]er invocationem solam septiformis Spiritus, episcopalis manus impositione." Siricius, *Epistula* 1.1.2, PL 13:1133. The English is ours.

14. Dale Sieverding, *The Reception of Baptized Christians: A History and Evaluation* (Chicago: Liturgy Training Publications, 2001), 5.

15. See Sieverding, *Reception of Baptized Christians*, 5–6; Paul Turner, *When Other Christians Become Catholic* (Collegeville, MN: Liturgical Press, 2007), 25. Sieverding has argued that what Innocent had in mind was the bestowal of the Holy Spirit and not canonical penance, but John Erickson argues that the distinction between canonical penance or confirmation is anachronistic for Innocent I. See John H. Erickson, "Divergences in Pastoral Practice in the Reception of Converts," in *Orthodox Perspectives on*

another regional synod near the Mediterranean coast of present-day France, not far from Arles, mandated the chrismation of heretics.[16] Pope Leo the Great (r. 440–461) advocated the laying on of hands and an invocation of the Holy Spirit[17] because baptisms outside of the church, while valid, lacked the consecrating power of the Spirit.[18] Faustus of Riez practiced chrismation,[19] and the Second Council of Arles (442–506) mandated the imposition of hands with chrism for Arians in canon 17,[20] and chrismation for heretics in danger of death in canon 26.[21] In the Western part

---

*Pastoral Praxis: Papers of Intra-Orthodox Conference on Pastoral Praxis (24-25 September 1986) Celebrating the 50th Anniversary of Holy Cross Greek Orthodox School of Theology (1937-1987)*, ed. Theodore Stylianopoulos (Brookline, MA: Holy Cross Orthodox Press, 1988), 155.

16. Orange can. 1, in *Concilia Galliae a. 314-506*, ed. Charles Munier, CCSL 148 (Turnhout: Brepols, 2001), 77–78. See Daniel Stramara, "Toward a Chrismatic Ecclesiology as a Theological Basis for Primacy," *Journal of Ecumenical Studies* 49, no. 2 (2014): 224; see also John Douglas Close Fisher, *Christian Initiation: Baptism in the Medieval West; A Study in the Disintegration of the Primitive Rite of Initiation*, Alcuin Club Collections No. 47 (London: SPCK, 1965), 31n139.

17. Leo the Great, *Epistula* 159.6-7, PL 54:1138–1339.

18. Turner, *When Other Christians Become Catholic*, 26; Sieverding, *Reception of Baptized Christians*, 6.

19. Faustus of Riez, *De gratia* 1.14, ed. Augustus Engelbrecht, CSEL 21 (Prague/Vienna/Leipzig: Tempsky/Freytag, 1891), 47.

20. II Arles can. 17, in *Concilia Galliae a. 314-506*, ed. Charles Munier, CCSL 148 (Turnhout: Brepols, 2001), 117.

21. II Arles can. 26, in *Concilia Galliae a. 314-506*, ed. Charles Munier, CCSL 148 (Turnhout: Brepols, 2001), 117. The canon appears to be a direct copy of Orange can. 1 (see above). It may be spurious: see Fisher, *Christian Initiation*, 31n139.

of the *oikumene*—as in the East—rites touching the skin were used to authenticate trinitarian baptism and faith, yet marked a threshold of ecclesial belonging.

Although the word "confirmation" is already used in Spanish documents, it seems to not so much imply the completion of initiation as the bishop's personal ratification of the ministry of priests on his behalf. In other words, in the west of the West this handlaying seems to be about the "grid" or internal hierarchy of the social body of the great church, not about its outer boundaries ("group"). Within this context, the reception of Novatians may similarly express primarily the proper relationship to the local bishop and his ecclesial communion. Novatians had rejected his authority by their rigid attitudes toward lapsed Christians, which was properly addressed by accepting his authoritative touch or chrism. In this sense, Novatians are recognized as inside the group of the catholic, orthodox church, but having an improper attitude toward its grid or exercise of hierarchy.

Since in this period there is a great deal of variety in initiatory practice in the West, it is often not possible to tell whether the sources that recommend chrismation or handlaying are imitating the contemporary initiatory practice. It would be anachronistic to conclude that the reception of repentant heretics is either a completion of their incomplete initiation or that it is not in any way initiatory, even when the prayer texts used are the same as those used for the post-baptismal rites.

Augustine's writings against the Donatists, in the end, made him the most influential authority in the West. He argued strongly that heretics and schismatics were validly baptized and simply had to be received through an imposition of hand, by which they were united to the church in the Holy Spirit's gift of charity.[22] The Donatists, like Cyprian, argued for rebaptism of those baptized outside the church; Augustine's position was most like Pope Leo's. For Augustine, the Spirit's gift of charity was recognized in the unity of the church.[23] The imposition of hands in their reception was not a "valid confirmation" substituting for an invalid one, but it did bestow the Holy Spirit, who awakened their love for their brothers and sisters.[24]

Severos of Antioch (465–538), a bishop in the non-Chalcedonian church in Syria, seems to have held basically the same theology.[25] He argued that the patriarchs of the Council of Ephesus allowed those who were estranged by schisms (not heresies) to be received by repudiating their schism.[26] Despite refusing the authority of Chalcedon, then, Severos and others turned to the

22. Augustine, *In Iohannis Evangelium Tractatus* 5.7, CCSL 36:44; *De baptismo* 5.24.33, CSEL 51:290; cf. also *De baptismo* 5.1.1, CSEL 51:261.

23. For a discussion on Augustine, see Sieverding, *Reception of Baptized Christians*, 5; Turner, *When Other Christians Become Catholic*, 24.

24. Augustine, *In Iohannis Evangelium* Tractatus 6.13-14, CCSL 36:60–61. For commentary, see Erickson, "Divergences," 156; Erickson, "Reception of Non-Orthodox Clergy into the Orthodox Church," *St. Vladimir's Theological Quarterly* 29 (1985): 70–72; Sieverding, *Reception of Baptized Christians*, 10–11.

25. For a discussion, see Erickson, "Divergences," 168.

26. Severos claimed that this practice of the imperial church was derived from behind-the-scenes decisions made at the Council of Ephesus. See Severus of Antioch, *The Sixth Book of the Select Letters of Severus, Patriarch of Antioch*, 2nd ed., ed. and trans. E. W. Brooks (Oxford: Clarendon, 1904), 348–49, 352–54. For a

Council of Ephesus (or its oral tradition) to establish the proper mode for the reconciliation of those outside the church.

The fifth century provides one example of how the fourth-century canons were received and implemented in the Byzantine church. An anonymous *Letter to Martyrios*, composed in the middle of the fifth century, seems to reveal the contemporary practice of the Great Church of Constantinople (i.e., Hagia Sophia).[27] It repeated the categories from the fourth-century canons, which seem to have been accepted as a "best practice" in fifth-century Constantinople. On the one hand, the *Letter* prescribed catechism and baptism for Eunomians, Montanists, and Sabellians (non-trinitarian sects)—converts from these sects are to be received "like heathens," the text reads. On the other hand, catechism-anathema-chrismation is prescribed for the reception of Arians, Macedonians, Novatians, Quartodecimans, and Apollinarians (sects with adequate trinitarian theologies). The chrismation

---

discussion, see John H. Erickson, "Reception of Non-Orthodox into the Church," *Diakonia* 19 (1984–1985), 78–80.

27. This letter was written from the imperial city to a patriarch in Antioch in response to his request about how to receive heretics into the church. The earliest extant copy of the letter appears in Syriac in a manuscript ca. 500. For an early Greek translation, see "Ἐπιστολὴ γραφεῖσα ἀπὸ Κωνσταντινουπόλεως Μαρτυρίῳ ἐπισκόπῳ Ἀντιοχείας, περὶ τοῦ, ὅπως χρὴ δέχεσθαι τοὺς αἱρετικοὺς προσερχομένους τῇ ἁγίᾳ καθολικῇ Ἐκκλησίᾳ," PG 119:900–901. The Syriac version can be found in *British Museum Addit. 14528*, ed. Friedrich Schulthess, *Die syrischen Kanones der Synoden von Nicaea bis Chalcedon nebst einigen zugehörigen Dokumenten herausgegeben* (Berlin: Weidmannsche, 1908), 145.

replicated the baptismal anointing with chrism, using the formula, "Seal of the gift of the holy Spirit."[28]

Another anonymous Byzantine text (ca. 450s) suggested that a baptism outside the church was in some way "repaired" by such a chrismation. *Quaestiones et responsiones ad Orthodoxos* presumed that the heretic's baptism was acceptable to the church but somehow —the author does not say how, exactly—in need of "making straight" or "fixing" (διορθεῖν).[29] Such "healing" models and metaphors for the reception of baptized Christians might provide an alternative to seeing them as repentant sinners or incompletely initiated.[30]

28. This Eastern formula was integrated into the Roman Rite only in the Vatican II reforms.

29. The Greek text can be found at *Quaestiones et responsiones ad Orthodoxos* 14, PG 6:1249–1400. For the latest scholarly consensus on dating and provenance, see Peter Toth, "New Questions on Old Answers: Towards a Critical Edition of the Answers to the Orthodox of Pseudo-Justin," *The Journal of Theological Studies*, New Series 65, no. 2 (October 2014): 550–99. Formerly the text was attributed to a Pseudo-Justin and transmitted among the works of Justin Martyr (ca. 100–165), but according to Toth the author actually may have been Theodoret of Cyr (393–457).

30. It is often forgotten that one of the key theologies of baptism is that of spiritual (and possibly physical) healing; see Robin Margaret Jensen, *Baptismal Imagery in Early Christianity: Ritual, Visual, and Theological Dimensions* (Grand Rapids, MI: Baker Academic/Baker Publishing Group, 2012), especially chapter 1. A connection between baptism and healing is also clear in some early sources. For example, in the fifth/sixth-century Alexandrian *Baptismal Ritual* from the Aksumite Collection there are rubrics for how to administer baptism to those who are sick (Alessandro Bausi, "The *Baptismal Ritual* in the Earliest Ethiopic Canonical Liturgical Collection," in »*Neugeboren aus Wasser und Heiligem Geist*« *Kölner Kolloquium zur Initiatio Christiana*, ed. Heinzgerd

By the seventh century, these models in East and West were crystallizing; by the eighth, they could be found in liturgical documents. In the Latin-speaking West, Gennadius of Marseilles (c. 490),[31] Gregory of Tours (538–594),[32] and Ildefonsus of Toledo (657–669)[33] seem to suggest that the imposition of the hand is given for some and imposition of hand with chrism for others, but they do not name the affected groups. The rite of reception appears to have had both a reconciliatory and an initiatory meaning.[34]

---

Brakmann, Tinatin Chronz, and Claudia Sode [Münster: Aschendorff Verlag, 2020], 75.20-26) and a reference to a post-baptismal anointing "for those who receive the washing and for the sick." Bausi, 79.26-27, with a prayer on 79.27-81.6.

31. Gennadius of Marseilles, *De ecclesiasticis dogmatibus* 52, PL 58:993.

32. Gregory of Tours, *Historia Francorum* 9.15, in *Gregorii Episcopi Turonensis, Libri Historiarum X*, 2nd ed., ed. Bruno Krusch and Wilhelm Levison, Monumenta Germaniae Historica, Scriptores Rerum Merovingicarum, vol. 1, tome 1 (Hannover: Hahn, 1965), 429.

33. Ildefonsus of Toledo, *De cognitione baptismi* 124 (121), in *Ildefonsi Toletani episcopi De virginitate Sanctae Mariae; De cognitione baptismi; De itinere deserti; De viris illustribus*, ed. Valeriano Yarza Urquiola and Carmen Codoñer Merino, CCSL 114A (Turnhout: Brepols, 2007), 419.

34. Sieverding has suggested that these two rituals were used interchangeably in Gaul in this time; see Sieverding, *Reception of Baptized Christians*, 6 and 122n24. However, caution is needed here, and these rituals are not exactly interchangeable and are likely better understood as ritual cognates. He has also suggested that Leo the Great, the texts from Gaul and Spain, and the practice in the East point to these rituals being associated with the initiatory bestowal of the Holy Spirit. If this is the case, this ritual perfected an imperfect baptism; see Sieverding, *Reception of Baptized*

Gregory the Great (d. 605), writing to the Spanish bishops, provides one of the most clear articulations of the reception of heretics and apostates at this time, though he is by no means describing a universal practice. As in the East, he draws distinctions between the various modes of reception—laying on of hands, chrismation, or a simple profession of faith—depending on the groups and local practice. However, the key distinction for Gregory regards trinitarian faith:

> We have taught from the ancient institution of the Fathers that those who are baptized in a heresy in the name of the Trinity, if they return to the Holy church, may be recalled to the womb of mother church either by the anointing of chrism, or by the imposition of the hand or by a mere profession of faith. For this reason, the West restores Arians to the door of the catholic church through the imposition of the hand, but the East through the anointing of sacred chrism.
>
> But the church receives Monophysites and others by a simple profession of faith because it accepts in them the holy baptism of cleansing, which they once pursued with the heretics. So either the former will have received the Holy Spirit through the imposition of the hand, or the latter will have been united to the heart of the holy and universal church through the profession of the true faith.[35]

---

*Christians*, 10 and 122n38–40. However, the material from Spain and Gaul is more ambiguous, as even Sieverding notes.

35. Gregory the Great, *Registrum Epistularum Libri VIII-XIV* 11.52, ed. Dag Norberg, CCSL 140A (Turnhout: Brepols, 1982), 952. The English is from Dale J. Sieverding, *Ordo admissionis valide iam baptizatorum in plenam communionem ecclesiae cath-*

Here we have an authoritative document from the central community which validates local practices, categorizes them, and characterizes them as equivalent to one another. By such category-making (grid) in the highest echelons, local practices are made interchangeable with one another.

A seventh-century Eastern treatise on the heresies, written by Timothy of Constantinople (a priest at Hagia Sophia),[36] reveals that the Great Church now knew a third possible mode of receiving heretics. That is, in addition to receiving some by rebaptism and some by anathema-chrismation (as in the *Letter to Martyrios*), others were received to the church's Eucharist after just an anathematization of heresy. This mode of reception to the church applied to those sects which rejected, for whatever reason, the teachings of the Third and Fourth Ecumenical Councils (i.e., Ephesus in 431 and Chalcedon in 451).

---

*olicae: An Historical Study of the Ritual Aspects of Reception into Full Communion with Special Attention to the Adaptations of the Rite for Use in the Catholic Church in the United States of America*, SLD diss. (Rome: Pontifical Liturgical Institute, 1997), 78.

36. Timothy the Presbyter, *De iis qui ad ecclesiam accedunt*, PG 8640C-68D. He also provides a list of all the contemporary non-Chalcedonian and non-Ephesian groups received in this way at Constantinople. See also Christiane Schmidt, "Timothy of Constantinople," in *Dictionary of Early Christian Literature*, ed. Siegmar Döpp and Wilhelm Geerlings, trans. Matthew O'Connell (New York: Herder and Herder, 2000), 579; against the accepted pre-Trullo dating, see Filippo Carcione, "Il 'De iis qui ad ecclesiam accedunt' del presbitero constantinopolitano Timoteo. Una nuova proposta di datazione," *Studi e ricerche dull'Oriente cristiano* 14 (1991): 309–20.

Trullo can. 95 has governed Byzantine reception ever since the seventh century; oddly, it exists because the fifth-century *Letter to Martyrios* was quoted as if it came from a much more authoritative document. The *Nomocanon of XIV Titles,* a seventh-century canonical manual, attributed the norm of baptism or chrismation taken from the *Letter* as the spurious Canon 7 of the Council of Constantinople (381).[37] This was a mistake, but one that significantly increased the impact of the *Letter*'s ritual prescriptions. Canon 2 of the Council *in Trullo* of Constantinople (691–692)[38] affirmed them and they formed the basis for Trullo can. 95, which summarized them, adding a prescription for receiving some heretics to the church by anathema alone.[39] In the end, Trullo can. 95 outlines three possible liturgical methods for the reception of heretics: rebaptism for Eunomians, Montanists, and Sabellians; first baptism for

37. There is no Canon 7 in the authentic *acta* of I Constantinople. Its first appearance was in the canonical manual *Nomocanon of XIV Titles,* ca. 610–641 CE, and it never entered the Western tradition. Peter L'Huillier, *The Church of the Ancient Councils: The Disciplinary Work of the First Four Ecumenical Councils* (Crestwood, NY: St. Vladimir's Seminary Press, 1996), 111; see also Louis Ligier, *La confirmation: sens et conjuncture oecuménique hier et aujourd'hui* (Paris: Beauchesne, 1973), 135–56.

38. For the Greek text, see Trullo can. 2, ed. George Nedungatt and Silvano Agrestini, CCCOGD 1:229–31. An English translation appears in "The Canons of the Council in Trullo," in *The Council in Trullo Revisited,* ed. George Nedungatt and Michael Featherstone, Kanonika 6 (Rome: Pontifical Oriental Institute, 1995), 64–69.

39. For the Greek text, see Trullo can. 95, ed. George Nedungatt and Silvano Agrestini, CCCOGD 1:287–89. An English translation appears in Nedungatt and Featherstone, "Canons of the Council in Trullo," 174–77.

Manicheans, Valentinians, and Marcionites; a written anathema and chrismation for Arians, Macedonians, Novatians, Quartodecimans, and Apollinarians; and a written anathema for Nestorians, Eutychians, and Severians. Trullo can. 95 still guides the reception of heretics—often called "converts" by the Orthodox today—into the Eastern Orthodox Churches.

## The Eighth-Century Emergence of Liturgical Texts

By the eighth century, then, when several Roman and Byzantine liturgical documents began to appear, their rituals received and implemented categories inherited from a variety of sources: ecumenical councils, local synods, and influential bishops. Rather than being established by one central authority, these categories were determined by persuasion, adoption of local synods' decisions, and perhaps even by historical error. In these rites, the least elaborate rituals were verbal professions and communion; the most elaborate were full initiation (baptism, with accompanying handlaying and chrismation, and communion). The intermediate rites of laying on of hands and chrismation could be interpreted in a variety of ways in both East and West. This ritual system managed the tension between recognizing the baptism of other Christian groups and ritualizing ecclesial belonging. Handlaying and chrismation affirmed baptism outside the boundaries of the great churches, but also supported, by the threshold established in touching the skin, claims to uniqueness and authority. Of course, up to this point there was no question of "receiving" Westerners into the Eastern

Church or vice versa. Though they were developing distinct ritual and theological traditions (grid), they saw one another as one body (group).

The first Roman liturgical text containing a rite of reception is the eighth-century Gelasian Sacramentary, which contains rites for the reception of Arians, heretics, and rebaptized apostates.[40] Unfortunately, these texts only contain the prayers and no rubrics, and so it is not clear what ritual gesture was used; however, the second half of each of the first and second prayers[41] are very similar to the prayer used in the post-baptismal liturgy in conjunction with the imposition of hands and mirrors the description of Pope Siricius's prayer.[42] This suggests that these were likely used with the imposition of hands. They also focus on the invocation of the Holy Spirit. The next set of prayers for the reconciliation of those rebaptized in heretical groups are much more penitential in tone and the gesture used cannot be determined, though an imposition of hand would seem most likely.[43] Perhaps the texts were already archaic and were meant to be adapted to unforeseen circumstances (hence the lack of rubrical clarity), as is clearly the case later in the Middle Ages (see chapter 4 below).

40. I.LXXXV-LXXXVII. Leo Cunibert Mohlberg, ed., *Liber sacramentorum Romanae aeclesiae ordinis anni circuli (Sacramentarium Gelasianum)* (Rome: Casa Editrice Herder, 1981), see §683–88.

41. I.LXXXV-LXXXVI.

42. For a summary of the discussion, see Turner, *When Other Christians Become Catholic,* 27–30; Sieverding, *Reception of Baptized Christians,* 13–17.

43. I.LXXXVII.

In the Byzantine Church, *Barberini gr. 336* (redacted 787–800 CE) contains a coherent Office for receiving heretics by chrismation.[44] In addition to substantially repeating the canonical norms of Trullo can. 95, the service also provided for a catechumenate culminating in the signing of a written anathema; a ritual in which the convert condemned their former heresy and professed faith in Christ, followed by chrismation on all the senses with the post-baptismal formula; and then admission to communion, followed by a week-long period of fasting which culminated in a ritual in which the remnants of the chrism were washed from the convert's body. The Office itself offered a very optimistic and affirmative perspective on Christian conversion. In its pre- and post-anointing prayers, the Byzantine Church affirmed that those being chrismated were already Christians, living a journey of faith in the incarnate and risen Lord—albeit "in error" and outside the "Orthodox fold."[45] This Office treated the chrismation of an already baptized convert with great "tolerance and benignity,"[46] that is, with an almost ecumenical sensitivity: this was the reconciliation of a

44. The Greek text can be found in *L'Eucologio Barberini gr. 336*, 2nd rev. ed., ed. Stefano Parenti and Elena Velkovska, BELS 80 (Rome: CLV Edizioni Liturgiche, 2000), 151–53; an Italian translation is given at 324–25.

45. According to John Klentos, who quotes the service. See Klentos, "Rebaptizing Converts into the Orthodox Church: Old Perspectives on a New Problem," *Studia Liturgica* 29 (1999): 228.

46. Miguel Arranz, "Évolution des rites d'incorporation et de readmission dans l'Église selon l'Euchologue byzantine," in *Gestes et paroles dans les diverses familles liturgiques: Conférences Saint-Serge XXIVe semaine d'études liturgiques (Paris 28 Juin — 1er*

baptized believer in Christ to the full truth of Christ in the church.[47]

Between the fourth and the eighth centuries, these local, tactical approaches to ecclesial ambiguities were gradually adapted into more centralized systems that maintained some recognition of baptisms in the name of the Trinity by trinitarian groups. The rites receiving such baptized persons were interpreted in various ways by different theologians, no doubt depending on local factors. With the increasing bureaucratic structures, however, the stage was set for a new type of ecclesial dispute: between the central authorities and their recalcitrant outlying provinces.

*Juillet 1977)*, ed. Achille Maria Triacca, BELS 14 (Rome: Centro Liturgico Vincenziano, 1978), 75.

47. Akliviadis C. Calivas, "Receiving Converts into the Orthodox Church: Lessons from the Canonical and Liturgical Tradition," in *The Liturgy in Dialogue: Exploring and Renewing the Tradition,* Essays in Liturgy and Theology 5 (Brookline, MA: Holy Cross Orthodox Press, 2018), 181–84.

# Chapter Four

# Rebaptism and Canonical Reinterpretation

## Trouble in Bulgaria: The Ninth-Century Conflict between East and West

The existence of fixed liturgical services for receiving baptized Christians in the Roman and Byzantine churches in the late antique period does not mean there were consistent practices. In fact, in the geopolitical and ecclesial borderlands between the Western and Eastern churches in the Middle Ages, the reception of baptized Christians became a major point of controversy. In the ninth century, there was a brief period of increased tension between East and West known as the "Photian schism" (863–867). In 860/861, Pope Nicholas I of Rome insisted that the former patriarch of Constantinople, Ignatios (ca. 793–877), had been deposed illegally. Ignatios had been removed and replaced with Photios I of Constantinople (810/820–893) by a synod convoked by Byzantine emperor Michael III (r. 842–867).[1] Rome

1. Francis Dvornik, *The Photian Schism: History and Legend* (Cambridge: Cambridge University Press, 1948), 76–80. Despite

also alleged that Photios had been raised much too quickly from the lay state to patriarch.[2] Nicholas's demands for a retrial led to a series of synods which rendered various conflicting decrees on the situation. Ultimately Nicholas declared Photios deposed (863), and Photios excommunicated Nicholas (867), before Photios himself was definitively deposed by a synod in Constantinople in 870.[3] Although these high-level conflicts were very visible, conflicts in the mission land of Bulgaria, including disputes over rebaptism of Christians, also played a role in the schism.[4]

Bulgaria, at this time, had significant missions from both Eastern and Western churches. East Frankish king

---

its age, this account remains the standard scholarly work on this groundbreaking conflict in the history of East-West relations.

2. Dvornik, *Photian Schism*, 76.

3. Photios was removed in favor of his opponent, and only upon Ignatios's death in 877 was Photios able to retake the patriarchal throne (finally unopposed by Rome). Andrew Louth, *Greek East and Latin West: The Church AD 681–1071*, The Church in History 3 (Crestwood, NY: St. Vladimir's Seminary Press, 2007), 186–87.

4. "In 858, Patriarch Ignatius had been deposed by Emperor Michael and replaced by Photius . . . When Ignatius' supporters appealed to Rome for support, Pope Nicholas I declared Photius' election invalid. When the latter refused to resign, Nicholas condemned and excommunicated the patriarch. In response to this unprecedented action, Photius convened a church council in 867 which condemned Pope Nicholas and terminated communion with Rome. This action was more than retaliation against Rome's refusal to recognize the patriarch: the deeper cause was the deteriorating situation in Bulgaria." Laurent Cleenewerck, *His Broken Body: Understanding and Healing the Schism between the Roman Catholic and Eastern Orthodox Churches: An Orthodox Perspective* (Washington, DC: Euclid University Consortium Press, 2007), 202–6.

Louis the German (r. 843–876) persuaded his ally King Boris I of Bulgaria (r. 852–889) to become a Christian. Instead of choosing Louis, a Latin Rite Christian, as his sponsor,[5] he chose Michael III, the Byzantine emperor.[6] Such an elite sponsor would probably have acted through a proxy rather than in person, yet the gesture of sponsorship was still politically vital and possibly dangerous. A sponsor had some authority over the person being baptized, and also lent some of the sponsor's protection and political legitimacy to the baptizand. Boris securing the emperor as a sponsor would advance his political goals, which fits our definition of a cultural survivalist.[7] From Boris's perspective, the emperor's validation of his baptism would also serve to authenticate his rule and his nation's sovereignty in

5. Louth, *Greek East and Latin West*, 180–81. Boris I of Bulgaria and the East Frankish king Louis the German (r. 843–876) had entered an alliance against Rastislav of Moravia (r. 846–870). As a result of this alliance, the Frankish king began to pressure Boris I to be baptized. Boris Todorov, "Coercion and Reconciliation: The Roman Mission of AD 866/7 and the Internal Conflicts in Bulgaria," in *Medieval Christianitas: Different Regions, "Faces," Approaches*, ed. Tsvetelin Stepanov and Georgi Kazakov (Sofia: "Mediaevalia Christiana," 2010), 182. See also J. M. Sansterre, "Les missionaires latins, grecs et orientaux en Bulgarie dans la seconde moitié du IXe siècle," *Byzantion: Revue internationale des études byzantines* 52 (1982): 375–88.

6. John V. A. Fine Jr., *The Early Medieval Balkans: A Critical Survey from the Sixth to the Late Twelfth Century* (Ann Arbor, MI: University of Michigan Press, 1983), 118.

7. From chapter 2 above: "Cultural survivalists or cosmopolitans, on the other hand, primarily act as individual agents that may traverse the boundaries between groups to achieve their own political goals."

the eyes of other Bulgarian leaders. Rome, on the other hand, was occupied by the higher-level conflict between East and West. From Pope Nicholas I's position, Boris's choice of a sponsor seemed to be a power play in the emerging Photian schism.

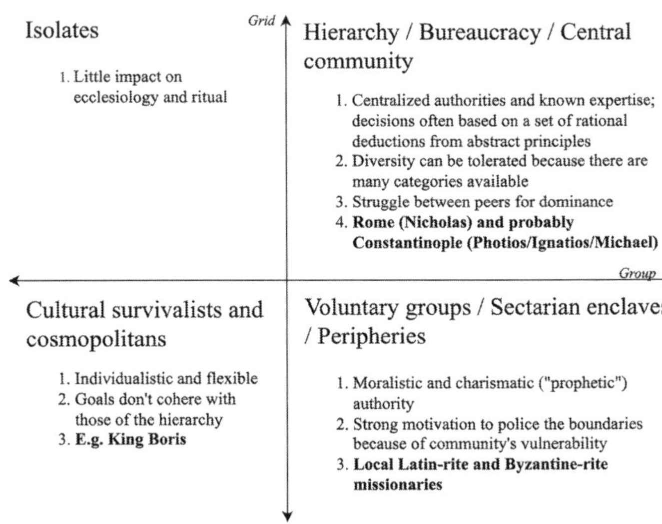


**Figure 4.1.** Representatives of each type of cultural community from the ninth-century Bulgarian controversy. Each axis represents a spectrum that might vary among representatives. Regular text summarizes the characteristics of each type of cultural community; bold text provides specific examples from this historical period.

The political ramifications of King Boris's baptism were not enough to prevent an ensuing revolt in Bulgaria. This likely motivated a reexamination of religious loyalties. In 866, the beleaguered king sent a delegation to Rome to meet with Pope Nicholas; the delegates brought with them a lengthy questionnaire on the Christian doctrine of Rome.[8] In response, Nicholas sent a delegation to Boris headed by Formosus of Porto and Paul of Populonia with the pope's 115 "Responsa." These answers to the king's theological and ritual inquiries are still extant, although the questionnaire is lost.[9] Boris seems to have asked under what conditions Christian baptism should be considered invalid, because in his *Responsum* 15 Nicholas confirms the validity of Byzantine baptisms.[10] In fact, "the pope's answers advised not to question baptisms even when performed by Jews and false priests."[11] The pope, writing from the center of Roman ecclesial power, repudiates rebaptism, but the inquiry about Roman policy suggests that some Latin priests in Bulgaria were rebaptizing Greek Christians.

Central communities, who judge from the peak of power and have a considerable information network,

8. Todorov, "Coercion and Reconciliation," 183. See more recently Tamás Nótári, "Some Remarks on the *Responsa Nicolai papae I. ad consulta Bulgarorum*," *Acta Univ. Sapientiae, Legal Studies* 4 (2015): 47–63. The questionnaire can be reconstructed; see I. Dujčev, "Die Responsa Papae Nicolai I ad consulta Bulgarorum als Quelle für die bulgarische Geschichte," in *Festschrift des Haus-, Hof- und Staatsarchivs*, vol. 1 (Vienna, 1949), 349–62.

9. Pope Nicholas I, *Responsa ad consulta Bulgarorum*, PL 119:978–1016.

10. "Sed in nomine summae ac individuae Trinitatis baptizati fuere, Christiani profecto sunt, et eos a quocunque Christiano baptizati sunt, iterato baptizare non convenit." Nicholas, *Responsa* 15, PL 119:986–87.

11. Todorov, "Coercion and Reconciliation," 191.

often see both cultural survivalists and dissenting enclaves as part of the whole bureaucratic organizational system. In this sense, King Boris is shopping around for an ecclesial ally who would effectively support his authority in Bulgaria; the local Latin missionaries, motivated to maximize the number of Bulgarians they are baptizing, treat Byzantine Christians as if they were pagans, in defiance of clear Roman norms. From the perspective of Rome, both the dissenting priests and King Boris fit into the larger tension with Constantinople. Nicholas's prime motivation is not Bulgarian national sovereignty. Rather, he is concerned, in classic bureaucratic style, with order: the proper administration of the sacraments and the respect due those sacraments by both churches.

Around the same time, a Byzantine letter similar to the pope's *Responsa* was sent to Boris, suggesting he had sent questionnaires to both Rome and Constantinople. In response, Photios "wrote a polemical treatise against Latin usages and dispatched it to the eastern patriarchs."[12] While Roman sources speak of rebaptizing, according to Photios's complaints in *Ep.* 2, other Latin priests were rechrismating Greek Christians.[13] Such rechrismation might have signified an ecclesiological rejection of the Byzantine church. A rite on the skin could reinforce social boundaries and call into question the theological legitimacy of Byzantine sacraments. Per-

12. Todorov, "Coercion and Reconciliation," 183.

13. Photios, *Epistula 2*, in *Photii Patriarchae Constantinopolitani Epistulae et Amphilochia*, ed. B. Laourdas and L. G. Westerink, vol. 1, *Epistularum Pars Prima*, Bibliotheca Scriptorum Graecorum et Romanorum Teubneriana (Leipzig: BSB B.G. Teubner Verlagsgesellschaft, 1983), 39–53, esp. 42–43.

haps, though, these rechrismations might simply have ensued on the basis of perceived differences in practice. After all, the Church of Rome insisted that confirmation be performed by the bishop, usually some time after the baptism, while Byzantine chrismation was performed by the priest at the baptism. Perhaps these rechrismations performed by the Latins in Bulgaria simply reflected a symbolic need, from the Western perspective, for the bishop's own hand to be laid on the initiand. On the other hand, perhaps rechrismation was a rejection of the chrism consecrated by Photios, because the circumstances surrounding the Photian schism may have rendered Photios's episcopacy illegitimate in the eyes of some Latin priests.

In fact, this seems confirmed by *Responsum* 94, which pertains directly to the validity of chrism: "You say that the Greeks claim that chrism originates in their country and by them is distributed to the whole world, and you therefore wish to know if this is true. Yet we believe that Your Cleverness has already noticed that it is not true."[14] The rumor on the street in Rome, clearly, was that Photios was distributing chrism and claiming

---

14. "Graecos dicere perhibetis, quod in illorum patria chrisma oriatur, et ab illis per totum mundum tribuatur: et ideo nosse desideratis, si verum sit: sed jam credimus quod vestra solertia quam verum non sit animadvertit." Nicholas, *Responsa* 94, PL 119:1012. The translation is adapted from W. L. North, "Medieval Sourcebook: The Responses of Pope Nicholas I to the Questions of the Bulgars A.D. 866 (Letter 99)," in *Internet Medieval Sourcebook*, last modified November 4, 2011, https://legacy.fordham.edu/Halsall /basis/866nicholas-bulgar.asp. See also G. T. Dennis, "The 'Anti-Greek' Character of the *Responsa Ad Bulgaros* of Nicholas I?," *Orientalia Christiana Periodica* 24 (1958): 171.

it as the only legitimate chrism. Perhaps Boris's question was a veiled reference to the Byzantine chrismation of Latin Christians in Bulgaria.

Based on Mary Douglas's work on the social body, A placing a hand on B's head suggests A has authority over B. This is one of the key embodied signifiers in ecclesiology, encoding hierarchy—that is, both A's power over and blessing for B. In both East and West, the chrism becomes the signifier at a distance of the power and blessing of the bishop, representing the symbolic touch of a bishop's hand, even when physically performed by a priest.[15] If the West insisted on the bishop's hand and the bishop's chrism as the central somatic signs of church unity, the East insisted on the patriarch's chrism: the proper patriarch was to send chrism consecrated by his hand to bishops and clergy throughout his church. The *Responsa* seems to have been among the earliest evidence of this norm.[16] The

15. Nathan Chase, "A Chrismatic Framework for Understanding the Intersection of Baptism and Ministry in the Roman Catholic and Eastern Churches," *Journal of Ecumenical Studies* 53 (2017): 319–67. See also Nathan Chase, "Oleoculture: The Production, Ritual Use, and Reservation of 'the Fruit of the Olive' in the Early Church," in *On Earth as in Heaven? Liturgy, Materiality, Economics*, ed. Melanie Ross (Collegeville, MN: Liturgical Press, 2025); Nathan Chase, "Anointings with Oil and Handlayings in the Early Western Church: Early Ritual Cognates?" (Öl in der frühen Liturgie: Verwendung und Deutung, Regensburg, February 9, 2024).

16. The reservation of the consecration of chrism to the patriarch or metropolitan appears to have begun in different times in the various Eastern churches: in the Armenian Church in the eighth century (today the catholicos of Cilicia and Etchmiadzin), among the Byzantine churches possibly as early as the ninth century (based on the witness of Photios) but certainly for sure by

claim that any valid chrism used in the Christian world came from Constantinople, then, would symbolically suggest that all true Christians had been touched on the head by the hand of the patriarch of Constantinople, who would consequently have authority over the whole Christian church.

After the Roman delegation's visit, Boris temporarily accepted Latin priests in the region and began expelling Byzantine priests, before definitively placing Bulgaria under Byzantine jurisdiction from 870 onward.[17] Throughout the late 860s, Boris had acted as an independent player in the emerging conflict between East and West—i.e., as a cultural survivalist—using the political consequences of the christianization of Bulgaria to his advantage. Unsurprisingly, however, the leadership of the Roman and Byzantine churches had

---

the thirteenth century, in the Coptic Church between the tenth and thirteenth centuries, and in the West Syrian tradition (but not East, which does not use chrism) around the twelfth/thirteenth century. For more, see E. Hermann, "Wann ist die Chrisamweihe zum ausschließlichen Vorrecht der Patriarchen geworden?," in *Recueil dédié à mémoire du prof. Peter Nikov* (Sofia: Blgarsko istorichesko druzhestvo, 1940), 509–15; Tinatin Chronz, Daniel Kölligan, and Heinzgerd Brakmann, "Die Feier der Myronweihe in der armenischen Kirche — mit einer deutschen Übersetzung und liturgiehistorischen Beobachtungen," *Oriens Christianus* 101 (2018): 177–79 and 207–8; Daniel F. Stramara Jr., "Toward a Chrismatic Ecclesiology as a Theological Basis for Primacy," *Journal of Ecumenical Studies* 49 (2014): 225–27; Heinzgerd Brakmann, "ⲂⲀⲡⲧⲓⲥⲙⲀ Ⲁⲓⲛⲉⲥⲉⲱⲥ: Ordines und Orationen kirchlicher Eingliederung in Alexandrien und Ägypten," in »*Neugeboren aus Wasser und Heiligem Geist*« *Kölner Kolloquium zur Initiatio Christiana*, ed. Heinzgerd Brakmann, Tinatin Chronz, and Claudia Sode (Münster: Aschendorff Verlag, 2020), 121–28 and 136–39.

17. Fine, *Early Medieval Balkans*, 124–25.

operated in Bulgaria from the perspective of central communities. They attempted to assert the normativity of their own bureaucracies by negotiating with Boris for the establishment of local hierarchies under their own respective jurisdiction,[18] as well as by sending missives informing Boris of their respective understandings of normative practices and doctrines. At the same time, Latin (and possibly Greek) missionaries operating in Bulgaria had functioned as sectarian enclaves. Even though there is manuscript evidence that both churches at this time possessed established rites for the reception of carefully defined groups of heretics and/or apostates,[19] Roman missionaries in Bulgaria—and perhaps Byzantine as well—were able to skirt these documented norms in order to delegitimize the ecclesial (and thus political) standing of members of the "rival" church by rebaptism and rechrismation.

The Bulgarian conflict thus illustrates the practical role of rites on the skin for establishing the boundaries of the ecclesial body in politically charged situations of conversion between churches. Ironically, by emphasizing the importance of the bishop's hand in ecclesial belonging (whether directly or through proper chrism), local actors could skirt hierarchical norms for receiving converts in their pursuit of desired social outcomes. Additionally, the Bulgarian conflict is an example in which it was more useful to the local

18. Cf. Fine, *Early Medieval Balkans*, 120–26.

19. For the Roman Church, in the eighth-century contents of the Old Gelasian Sacramentary (Vatican Reginensis 316); for the Byzantine Church, in the eighth-century "Barberini Euchologion" (*Barberini gr. 336*), among others. See the discussions above.

Bulgarian enclaves to have ritual texts for receiving converts that had outdated and inapplicable categories. Because the categories of heretics in these texts did not include members of the "rival" church, Latin priests could choose to apply the Roman norm (chrismation) for Arians in the Old Gelasian Sacramentary to the "transfer" of Eastern Christians into the Western ecclesial structure. For local actors, that is, these now-fictional categories allowed for improvisation that evaded Rome's authority over its rites.

## Late Medieval and Early Modern Developments

By the late Middle Ages, there were two different Western approaches for receiving baptized Christians. The first approach nominally applied to Arians, heretics, and apostates—again, increasingly rare categories—and appeared in official liturgical books. The second approach centered upon the fact that no rite was explicitly developed for the reception of Eastern Christians until Vatican II. Instead, the Western dioceses developed practices for receiving Eastern Christians that often mirrored the rituals for the reception of Arians, heretics, and apostates. The lack of an official ritual for receiving Eastern Christians allowed for adaptation as the political relationship changed, but also allowed local clergy to ignore Roman stipulations about the validity of Eastern initiation. In some cases, members of the Byzantine Church entering communion with the Western Church were compelled to make a special profession of faith. For example, the reunion rite for Byzantine emperor Michael Palaeologus (r. 1261–1282) was recycled a century later for a group of Byzantine Christians who entered communion with Rome in 1385.[20] Thus the central community at Rome enacted a ritual means for reception which marked the social boundaries of the church, but in the softest manner possible.

The Council of Ferrara-Florence (1438–1441) was convened to address the schisms between the East and West.[21] The emperor and bishop delegates from the East desired reunion, but the doctrinal compromises of the council were not acceptable to Byzantine Christians. Not long after the council closed, Constantinople fell to the Ottoman Empire in 1453. The bull *Exsultate Deo* ("Decree for the Armenians," Council of Florence, 1439), however, laid the groundwork for an eventual reconciliation between the Armenian Church and Rome.[22] The delegate for the Armenian patriarch formally acquiesced to the decree and an abjuration

20. For the sources, see Joseph G. Goodwine, *The Reception of Converts: Commentary with Historical Notes*, Canon Law Studies 198 (Washington, DC: The Catholic University of America Press, 1944), 120.

21. This council began in Basel in 1431 and ended in 1444; these dates represent the dates of participation by both Eastern and Western bishops.

22. This formally happened in 1742, when Pope Benedict XIV "confirmed" a bishop of the Armenian Apostolic Church—i.e., Oriental Orthodox—as the (Catholic) patriarch of some small scattered Armenian Christian communities in communion with Rome. See Ronald G. Roberson, *The Eastern Christian Churches: A Brief Survey*, 5th ed. (Rome: Edizioni Orientalia Christiana, 1995), 131. For the critical edition of the decrees of the Council of Ferrara-Florence, see "1437-1445: Ferrara-Florence-Rome," in *The General Councils of Latin Christendom: From Constantinople IV (869/870)–Lateran V (1512–1517)*, vol. 2, CCCOGD 2/2 (Turnhout: Brepols, 2013).

of doctrines opposed by Rome, though it is unclear what rituals (if any) were meant to follow in Armenia.

Similarly, in the Eastern churches of Byzantine provenance, no official rite was explicitly composed for the reception of Western Christians until the fifteenth century. Rather, the categories from Trullo can. 95, which specified reception by written anathema or anathema and chrismation, were applied. In the latter case, perhaps these Christians would have been received in the Byzantine Church according to the liturgical rite found in *Barberini gr. 336*, mentioned earlier. Following the failure of the Council of Florence, however, a 1484 council in Constantinople, which was attended by all four Eastern patriarchs and which repudiated the failed union of Ferrara-Florence, developed a specific rite and canonical status for the reception of Western Christians, whom the Eastern Orthodox Church received by anointing them with chrism.[23] We will return to this service in detail at the end of this chapter.

## "Arians, Heretics, and Apostates": The Western Liturgical Books of the Middle Ages

The threat from Arianism and other ancient heresies had largely ceased in the West after the official

---

23. See George D. Dragas, "The Manner of Reception of Roman Catholic Converts into the Orthodox Church with Special Reference to the Decisions of the Synods of 1484 (Constantinople), 1755 (Constantinople) and 1667 (Moscow)," *Greek Orthodox Theological Review* 44, no. 1–4 (1999): 238–242. See also Akliviadis C. Calivas, "Receiving Converts into the Orthodox Church: Lessons from the Canonical and Liturgical Tradition," in *The Liturgy in Dialogue: Exploring and Renewing the Tradition*, Essays in Liturgy and Theology 5 (Brookline, MA: Holy Cross Orthodox Press, 2018), 184–87.

conversion of the Visigothic Kingdom in the sixth century,[24] but rubrics for how to deal with "Arians, heretics, and apostates" were still included in Roman, Gallican, and Hispano-Mozarabic liturgical books. The tenth-century Romano-Germanic Pontifical (PRG), likely redacted in Mainz for services celebrated by a local bishop, recycled the same prayers that earlier appeared in the Old Gelasian Sacramentary.[25] In the PRG, however, it is clear that they would be accompanied by an imposition of hands.[26] The PRG titles for the prayers prescribe a "blessing with an imposition of hands" for converted heretics[27] and a "reconciliation with an imposition of hands" for a former Christian reverting from paganism (an apostate).[28] The title of a reconciliation prayer for "a person rebaptized by heretics" does not provide rubrical indications, al-

24. Nathan Chase, "From Arianism to Orthodoxy: The Role of the Rites of Initiation in Uniting the Visigothic Kingdom," *Hispania Sacra* 72:146 (2020): 427–38.

25. Dale Sieverding, *The Reception of Baptized Christians: A History and Evaluation* (Chicago: Liturgy Training Publications, 2001), 19. See *Sacramentarium Gelasianum*: Leo Cunibert Mohlberg, ed., *Liber sacramentorum Romanae aeclesiae ordinis anni circuli (Sacramentarium Gelasianum)* (Rome: Casa Editrice Herder, 1981), §683–88.

26. Scholars believe that the Gelasian Sacramentary also would likely have included a handlaying, but it is not explicitly indicated in the text. See the discussion in chapter 2 above, p. 64.

27. "Benedictio cum impositione manuum super eos qui de diversis heresibus veniunt." Cyrille Vogel and Reinhard Elze, *Le Pontifical romano-germanique du dixième siècle*, vol. 2, *Le Texte. II (nn. XCIC-CCLVII)*, *Studi e Testi* 227 (Vatican City: Biblioteca Apostolica Vaticana, 1963), §CCXVI.

28. "Reconciliatio cum impositione manuum redeuntis a paganis." Vogel and Elze, *Pontifical romano-germanique*, §CCXVII.

though it may also have included a handlaying.[29] The rite does not include chrism or an anointing.[30] Heretics are not classified by name—Arians, for instance, are not mentioned—but grouped together, just as in the Gelasian Sacramentary. One handlaying on the skin was judged by the redactors of this pontifical as adequate to establish the distance from the social body of all these received groups.

In Iberia, special regulations for Jews and Muslims who converted were increasingly placed alongside those for "heretics and apostates" in the rites of initiation,[31] because Muslims and especially Jews were now viewed as the primary local threat to ecclesial self-identity.[32] In the Visigothic Kingdom and Carolingian Empire, baptism and ecclesial belonging were central to the construction of a homogenous society; the inclusion of Jews in rites to address issues in the social body was ecclesiologically incoherent, but sociologically convenient.[33] Similarly, Islam had become a

---

29. "Reconciliatio rebaptizati ab hereticis." Vogel and Elze, *Pontifical romano-germanique*, §CCXXIV.

30. See the discussion of this rite on p. 64. For a commentary, see Sieverding, *Reception of Baptized Christians*, 19.

31. See, for instance, Chase, "From Arianism to Orthodoxy," 431–32.

32. Jewish converts, in particular, were often thought to be on the verge of apostasy: see Nathan Chase, *The* Homiliae Toletanae *and the Theology of Lent and Easter*, Spicilegium Sacrum Lovaniense, Études et Documents 56, Studia Breviora 2 (Leuven: Peeters, 2020), 62–64. Interestingly, meals between these groups were highly regulated.

33. Chase, "From Arianism to Orthodoxy"; Owen Michael Phelan, *The Formation of Christian Europe: The Carolingians, Baptism, and the Imperium Christianum* (Oxford: Oxford University Press, 2014).

major threat with the invasion of North Africa and the Iberian Peninsula, and so the boundary rites included Muslims as well. Only after the Second Vatican Council would these groups cease to be named in the rubrics and texts within liturgical books.

Within the ecclesiologically challenging territories of Iberia, then, we see a unique set of rites for reception from those in the Gelasian Sacramentary tradition. The eleventh-century Hispano-Mozarabic *Liber Ordinum* (LO)[34] contains a rite for the reconciliation of Arians, a rite for the reception of an apostate Christian who submitted to rebaptism in a heretical sect, and a prayer over converted Jews.[35] The exact date of the *Liber Ordinum* is a source of ongoing speculation. The rite for the reconciliation of the Arians reflects a practice (imposition and chrism) instituted by Canon 17 of the Second Council of Arles (442–506), which was then part of Visigoth Spain. The oldest extant manuscript of LO is from the eleventh century, but the rite likely reflects seventh-century reforms and expansions of the Hispano-Mozarabic Rite.[36] Even in the seventh century, the inclusion of Arians would be somewhat anachronis-

34. For a commentary on the relevant rites from this text, see Paul Turner, *When Other Christians Become Catholic* (Collegeville, MN: Liturgical Press, 2007), 30–33; Sieverding, *Reception of Baptized Christians,* 17–18.

35. The standard edition cited by most scholars is that of Marius Férotin, Anthony Ward, and Cuthbert Johnson, *Le liber ordinum: en usage dans l'église wisigothique et mozarabe d'espagne du cinquième au onzième siècle,* Réimpr. de l'éd. 1904 et suppl. de bibliographie générale de la liturgie hispanique, BELS 83 (Rome: C. L. V. - Edizioni Liturgiche, 1996). These rites appear at §100–107.

36. Chase, "From Arianism to Orthodoxy," 427–38.

tic, as the kingdom had converted to the Nicene faith about a century earlier. The oldest complete Western *ordo* for receiving a validly baptized Christian, it takes the form of a verbal renunciation and adherence ceremony, followed by two ritual actions performed on the skin (chrismation and imposition of hand).

In the rite, the candidate renounces the heretical trinitarian teachings of Arianism and confesses the unity of the three divine persons. Then, he or she is anointed with chrism: "And I chrismate [*chrismo*] you in the name of the Father and the Son and the Holy Spirit, in remission of all your sins, in order that you may have eternal life. Amen."[37] The connection between the trinitarian renunciation-adherence, on the one hand, and the trinitarian chrismation formula with its absolution from sin, on the other, is striking; it suggests a dependence upon similar liturgical structures in the initiation rites.[38] The rite concludes with an imposition of hands during the "prayer of confirmation" (titled *oratio confirmationis*), which mentions the seven gifts of the Holy Spirit.[39] This prayer, a variant of the oration of baptismal chrismation in LO,[40] should not be assumed to bear the same theological meaning that the sacrament of confirmation has today in the Roman Catholic Church.[41] Despite a valid baptism, both a

37. "Et ego te chrismo in nomine Patris et Eilii, et Spiritus Sancti, in remissione omnium peccatorum, ut habeas vitam eternam. Amen." Férotin, Ward, and Johnson, *Le liber ordinum*, §100–103.

38. Sieverding, *Reception of Baptized Christians*, 18.

39. Férotin, Ward, and Johnson, *Le liber ordinum*, §100–103.

40. Sieverding, *Reception of Baptized Christians*, 18.

41. Turner, *When Other Christians Become Catholic*, 32–33.

verbal ritual related to the heresy itself (renunciation-adherence) and two separate rites on the skin (chrismation and imposition of hand) were judged necessary to permit the (fictional) former Arian to pass across the boundaries of the social body. In the same way that Easterners were assimilated to pagans in Bulgaria, those outside the church in Iberia (even Jews and Muslims, or those who had converted to these faiths) were assimilated to Arians, heretics, and apostates.

Nearly simultaneous with the manuscript of the LO is the eleventh-century *Rivipullense* sacramentary, which reflects the Catalonia-Narbonne liturgical tradition.[42] This sacramentary displays a mixture of Hispano-Mozarabic and Roman features and contains a single "*Ordo* for reconciling an apostate converted from Judaism, heresy, or paganism."[43] The pastoral circumstances for which this ritual was composed are not entirely clear, especially since the terms "heretic" and "apostate" seem to be used synonymously in the service.[44] It appears that the redactor of this *ordo* did,

42. For more on the liturgical tradition in Catalonia-Narbonne, see Nathan Chase, "A Frayed Tapestry: The Future of the Western Non-Roman Rites," *Questions Liturgiques/Studies in Liturgy* 101 (2021): 39.

43. Alejandro Olivar, *Sacramentarium Rivipullense*, Monumenta Hispaniae Sacra, Serie Liturgica VII (Madrid: Instituto Enrique Flórez, 1964), §1422–29. The title of this rite reads: "Ordo ad reconciliandum apostatam a iudaismo, haeresi vel gentilitate."

44. Turner, *When Other Christians Become Catholic*, 33. As he further notes: "It is not clear whether this was intended for a true apostate, in the sense of one individual who began life as a faithful Christian, or if the term at this time and place more broadly applied to the group of those outside Christianity."

however, presuppose a valid baptism. The bishop was to bless water, breathe on the candidate three times, exorcize him or her, and then permit his or her entrance into the church. Inside, the candidate prostrated on the floor while the penitential psalms were prayed, followed by the *Kyrie*, Lord's Prayer, *Salvum fac*, and two prayers for reconciling apostates (adopted from the Gellone Sacramentary, a Gallican book).[45] The candidate would then renounce Satan, be signed with chrism, be assigned a penance, and finally receive the Eucharist.[46] The *Rivipullense* does not contain an imposition of hands, and its use of a penance is unprecedented in the reception of such a "heretic" or "apostate."

The reception *ordo* in the *Rivipullense* sacramentary would eventually have an outsize effect on subsequent Western Catholic tradition. But this *ordo* was not immediately adopted into the pontifical tradition. Until the end of the thirteenth century, pontificals in Europe contained neither the orations for heretics from older sacramentaries nor even an *ordo* for receiving heretics.[47] Given the sociopolitical climate of contemporary Western Europe, this might indicate that their redactors did not see a need for such *ordines*. William Durandus, however, bishop of Mende in France (r. 1285–1296), used a copy of the *Rivipullense* rite when

45. The *Liber Sacramentorum Gellonensis*, ed. Antoine Dumas and Jean Deshusses, CCSL 159A (Turnhout: Brepols, 1981), §2395–96.

46. For a discussion, see Turner, *When Other Christians Become Catholic*, 33; Sieverding, *Reception of Baptized Christians*, 18. Sieverding includes an imposition of hands, but a look at the *Rivipullense* sacramentary reveals that he is wrong.

47. Sieverding, *Reception of Baptized Christians*, 19.

creating the "Rite for reconciling apostates, schismatics, or heretics" in his famous Pontifical (PWD), in addition to adapting parts of the baptismal ritual for the use of converts.[48] Then, the liturgical reformers implementing the Council of Trent received a version of the *Rivipullense* rite into the *Pontificale Romanum* of 1595 by way of the PWD.[49]

The rite in the PWD is based on the *Rivipullense* rite, but it collapses the treatment of heretics, schismatics, and apostates into one ritual category, creating a unified rite to deal with all the anomalies in the social body.[50] The formal entrance into the church follows some initial ceremonies: an interrogation, an exorcism taken almost verbatim from *Rivipullense*, and

48. Pontifical of Wiliam Durandus 3.9, in Michel Andrieu, *Le Pontifical romain au moyen âge*, vol. 3, *Le Pontifical de Guillaume Durand* (Vatican City: Bibliotheca Apostolica Vaticana, 1940), 616–19. Dale J. Sieverding, *Ordo admissionis valide iam baptizatorum in plenam communionem ecclesiae catholicae: An Historical Study of the Ritual Aspects of Reception into Full Communion with Special Attention to the Adaptations of the Rite for Use in the Catholic Church in the United States of America*, SLD diss. (Rome: Pontifical Liturgical Institute, 1997), 139.

49. Sieverding, *Historical Study*, 135–36 and footnotes. For the edition, see Manlio Sodi and Achille M. Triacca, *Pontificale Romanum: editio princeps: 1595–1596*, Edizione anastatica, Monumenta liturgica Concilii Tridentini 1 (Vatican City: Libreria Editrice Vaticana, 1997).

50. Cf. Turner, *When Other Christians Become Catholic*, 35. But on page 37, Turner notes, "It is possible that Durandus meant for the bishop to read certain parts of the text with one of three options. For example, he might have intended this prayer [during the imposition] to mention pagans, heresy, or Judaism, but not all three. Most likely, though, a bishop who wanted a pontifical in front of him would read all the words on the page."

a signing. The signing is reminiscent of the one in the PWD initiation rites, but the prayer while entering is an adaptation from a similar oration in the *Rivipullense*.[51] A second oration to conclude the entrance is taken directly from the Gelasian tradition for the "reconciliation of someone rebaptized by heretics."[52] Next follows a three-part interrogation of the candidate as to whether they profess the faith of the Creed (and which is similar to the interrogation in the initiation *ordo*).[53] The subsequent renunciation of Satan is highly reminiscent of that in the *Rivipullense*, and includes the question: "Do you also renounce every pagan sect, heretical distortion, or Jewish superstition?"[54]

Unlike the Spanish source, however, the PWD rite omits an anointing with chrism, prescribing only an imposition of hands during the prayer with the classic "sevenfold gifts" of the Spirit, as in the prayer at confirmation.[55] Nevertheless, omitting a chrismation

51. Sieverding, *Historical Study*, 141; PWD 3.9, in Andrieu, *Pontifical romain*, 3:616–17.

52. "Reconciliatio rebaptizati ab heredicis," in *Sacramentarium Gelasianum*, ed. Mohlberg, §687; it also appears in the Gallican sacramentary tradition in the *Liber Sacramentorum Gellonensis*, ed. Dumas and Deshusses, §2395.

53. Sieverding, *Reception of Baptized Christians*, 20.

54. "Abrenuntias etiam omni secte gentilitatis vel heretice pravitatis sive iudaice superstitionis?," PWD 3.9, in Andrieu, *Pontifical romain*, 3:617. The English is from Turner, *When Other Christians Become Catholic*, 36.

55. The prayer itself is quite similar to the equivalent found in Roman sources, Gallican books, and the *Rivipullense*. See *Sacramentarium Gelasianum*, ed. Mohlberg, §684–85; *Liber Sacramentorum Gellonensis*, ed. Dumas and Deshusses, §2394, 2396; Olivar, *Sacramentarium Rivipullense*, §1427. For a discussion, see Sieverding, *Historical Study*, 144.

and including a prayer focused on the reconciliation of an apostate prevents an easy identification of this ritual with the rite of confirmation.[56] Despite the source material in the *Rivipullense*, the PWD prioritizes hand-laying, the gesture which had generally been privileged in the West for the reception of heretics since at least the fifth century.

The oration that accompanied the *impositio* seems to have been equally applicable for the reception of a heretic or the reconciliation of an apostate.[57] The ritual abjurations which conclude the service also involved the renunciations of schism and of heresy, respectively.[58] Despite the differences in their relation to the ecclesial body, the PWD treats the reception of heretics, schismatics, and apostates without distinction. This may be due in part to the influence of the *Rivipullense* sacramentary. Paradoxically, the rite has an undertone of reconciliation, which was achieved by adapting the rites of initiation. Durandus evidently wanted to evoke the relationship of the valid baptisms of these heretics and apostates to the church's initiation rites.

Interpolating a rite for the reconciliation of heretics or apostates that had been absent in earlier liturgical books suggests that there was a need for such a ritual,

---

56. For a discussion, see Turner, *When Other Christians Become Catholic*, 33–37; Sieverding, *Reception of Baptized Christians*, 19–21.

57. "Domine Deus omnipotens, pater domini nostri Iesu Christi, qui dignatus es hunc famulum tuum ab errore gentilitatis vel mendacio heretice pravitatis sive iudaice superstitionis clementer eruere et ad ecclesiam tuam sanctam revocare, tu, domine, emitte in eum spiritum sanctum paraclitum de celis." PWD 3.9, in Andrieu, *Pontifical romain*, 3:617–18.

58. PWD 3.9, in Andrieu, *Pontifical romain*, 3:618–19.

likely for apostates rather than for heretics.[59] The issue was no longer with historical heretical sects, such as the ancient Donatists or Arians; now the church saw a threat in extra-ecclesial groups, namely Jews and Muslims, to whom some Christians were perceived to have apostatized. On the western edges of the Western Church, distinct rituals for heretics and apostates were no longer especially necessary, because the tiny heretical groups in this period were not perceived to be a real political threat. Thus an abjuration, handlaying, and invocation of the Spirit were judged to be enough to effect the passage of an alienated Christian across the boundary of the social body into the church. Indeed, in the 1485 *Editio princeps* of the *Pontificale Romanum*, based on the PWD, this rite was omitted. The intense intra- and extra-ecclesial evolutions of the Reformation, however, motivated its recovery and insertion into the Tridentine *Pontificale Romanum*.[60]

59. For some of the background on heresy in this period, see Brenda Bolton, "Tradition and Temerity: Papal Attitudes to Deviants, 1159–1216," in *Schism, Heresy and Religious Protest*, ed. Derek Baker (Cambridge: Cambridge University Press, 1972), 79–91. See also the other chapters in the volume. Curiously, in the *Editio princeps* of the *Pontificale Romanum* published in 1485 and based on the PWD, this *ordo* was removed. Sieverding suggests its omission was because it was of little use, but this period was marked by problems with Wycliffe and Hus. See, for instance, Michael Wilks, "Reformatio Regni: Wyclif and Hus as Leaders of Religious Protest Movements," in *Schism, Heresy and Religious Protest*, ed. Derek Baker (Cambridge: Cambridge University Press, 1972), 109–30.

60. The ongoing relevance of this rite is surely a result of the Reformation. Sieverding, *Reception of Baptized Christians*, 126n25.

## East-West Relations in the "Medieval" Period

Meanwhile, in the East, the seventh-century Trullo can. 95 continued to be adapted to a shifting ecclesiological world. The canon implied that some baptisms were acceptable to the Orthodox Church even though they were performed by outside groups, but it did not provide theological motives for its classification into now-defunct late antique heretical groups.[61] Consequently, ongoing interpretation was needed: for each potential convert coming from the West, Byzantine theologians and canonists had to identify which canonical category was most analogous to their ecclesial group. For instance, Methodios I of Constantinople (r. 843–847) had to decide how to receive repentant Iconoclasts after their condemnation at the Seventh Ecumenical Council, II Nicaea (843). Since the council likened Iconoclasm to Arianism (both heresies were considered defective views of Christ's incarnation), Methodios chose to receive Iconoclasts by an anathema and chrismation,[62] just as Trullo can. 95 had prescribed for Arians. The recognition of a theological boundary between the church community and the out-group required a strong rite on the skin, and could be justified in accordance with the canons.

61. David Heith-Stade, "Receiving the Non-Orthodox: A Historical Study of Greek Orthodox Canon Law," *Studia Canonica* 44, no. 2 (2010): 400–401.

62. Methodios I of Constantinople, *Testament*, quoted in Nicetas of Heraclea, *On the Heresiarchs*, text edited in *Documents inédits d'ecclésiologie byzantine*, ed. Jean Darrouzès, Archives de l'Orient Chrétien 10 (Paris: Institut Français d'Études Byzantines, 1966), 292–95.

Likewise, canonists had to decide into which category Latin Christians fell: chrismation or simple anathema. Some chose the latter, such as Theodore Balsamon (d. 1195), who argued that despite evident differences in customs the churches remained very similar in their essential beliefs.[63] Others, such as Mark of Ephesus (1392–1444), argued that the theological differences were much more drastic. Much like Methodios with the Iconoclasts, Mark compared the Latin heresy of the *filioque* to Arianism.[64] For Mark, this necessitated the reception of Latins by anathema and chrismation.[65] Of course, some local decision makers chose to rebaptize Latin converts.[66] This could be justified with polemics against Latin non-immersion baptism, which had some basis in the canonical tradition ("Apostolic Canon" 50).[67] Here, again, enclave-like suspicion of the primary

63. Patrick D. Viscuso, *Guide for a Church Under Islām: The Sixty-Six Canonical Questions Attributed to Theodōros Balsamōn: A Translation of the Ecumenical Patriarch's Twelfth-Century Guidance to the Patriarch of Alexandria* (Brookline, MA: Holy Cross Orthodox Press, 2014), 33, 106.

64. That is, whereas the original Nicene-Constantinopolitan Creed said that the Spirit "proceeds from the Father," the Western Church said "proceeds from the Father *and the Son [filioque]*."

65. Kallistos Ware, "The Rebaptism of Heretics in the Orthodox Canonical Tradition," in *Heresy and the Making of European Culture: Medieval and Modern Perspectives*, ed. Andrew P. Roach and James R. Simpson (London: Taylor and Francis, 2013), 43.

66. Timothy (= Kallistos) Ware, *Eustratios Argenti: A Study of the Greek Church under Turkish Rule* (Oxford: Clarendon, 1964), 66; J. R. Ryder, "Changing Perspectives on 1054," *Byzantine and Modern Greek Studies* 35, no. 1 (2011): 25–29.

67. Calivas, "Receiving Converts," 152–53; Tia M. Kolbaba, *The Byzantine Lists: Errors of the Latins* (Urbana/Chicago: University of Illinois Press, 2000), 3, 43.

out-group (in this case, Latin Christians) overrode the authoritative canonical interpretations, and local communities stipulated more intense rituals on the skin of received Christians than the recognized experts required.

In the West, meanwhile, a similar rebaptism controversy emerged in present-day Poland, Lithuania, Ukraine, and the Balkans, where Latin and Byzantine ecclesial influence converged.[68] The rebaptism of Orthodox Christians was consistently forbidden by the central authorities at Rome, who decreed the reception of Orthodox through a confession of faith alone. However, the fourteenth-century Hungarian and Polish monarchies tried to "assimilate 'schismatics' with pagans, and therefore, rebaptize Orthodox converts."[69] Local communities under their monarchies acted as dissenting enclaves, ignoring their own central community's rules in advocating more intense rituals of reception. The rebaptism of the Orthodox by Latin clergy appears to have begun with King Louis of Hungary (r. 1342–1382), who conquered Vidin in western Bulgaria in 1365.[70] Louis also allowed for the rebap-

68. For a helpful look at the political and religious situation of the Baltic Frontier around the time of the Great Schism, see Alan V. Murray, ed., *The Clash of Cultures on the Medieval Baltic Frontier* (Burlington: Ashgate, 2009); Jean W. Sedlar, "Religion and the Churches," in *A History of East Central Europe: East Central Europe in the Middle Ages, 1000–1500*, vol. 3 (London: University of Washington Press, 1994), 140–96.

69. John Meyendorff, *Byzantium and the Rise of Russia: A Study of Byzantino-Russian Relations in the Fourteenth Century* (New York: Cambridge University Press, 1981), 243.

70. John Meyendorff notes that this was "not officially condoned in Rome, and the popes of the fourteenth and fifteenth centuries

tism of Orthodox in Transylvania.[71] At the same time, Louis and his mother Elisabeth of Poland demanded that John V of the Byzantine Empire convert to Catholicism. Urban V intervened and said that John V should not be rebaptized but only profess an oath to Rome.[72] Despite this, the Hungarians rebaptized Prince Stracimir of Bulgaria and many of his subjects.[73] In 1370 Casimir III the Great of Poland threatened to baptize the Russians of Galicia.[74] The Franciscan Vicar of Bosnia also forbade rebaptism in a letter in 1379, implying that the practice was occurring there too.[75] In 1386 Jacob-Jagiello, then Duke of Lithuania and the future king of Poland, was rebaptized. There seems to have been an especial temptation, from an enclave perspective, to rebaptize royal figures, as they symbolically represent the whole of the threatening outside group.

In Poland during the fifteenth and sixteenth centuries, this controversy continued. Again the papal court validated Orthodox baptism, while the local Polish Catholic episcopate and theologians at Krakow

---

always accepted Orthodox converts to the Roman communion through a simple confession of faith, recognizing the 'validity' of their Orthodox baptism; but the papacy generally encouraged the Crusading spirit of the Hungarians and the Poles." Meyendorff, "Projets de Concile Oecuménique en 1367: Un dialogue inédit entre Jean Cantacuzène et le légat Paul," *Dumbarton Oaks Papers* 14 (1960): 154. Henceforth Meyendorff, "Projets." Translation by Nathan Chase.

71. Sedlar, "Religion and the Churches," 170.

72. Meyendorff, "Projets," 155; Meyendorff, *Byzantium and the Rise of Russia*, 66.

73. Meyendorff, *Byzantium and the Rise of Russia*, 66.

74. Meyendorff, *Byzantium and the Rise of Russia*, 67.

75. Meyendorff, *Byzantium and the Rise of Russia*, 66n51.

University required rebaptism. Unlike other local enclaves, this eventually led to outright dissidence between the Polish episcopate and the papal court.[76] The issue was brought to the Council of Constance in 1417 without result.[77] Although some Polish theologians argued against rebaptism of Ruthenian Christians,[78] rebaptism of the Orthodox Ruthenians continued throughout the fifteenth century as the local Latin hierarchy and several synods and dioceses insisted on rebaptism. In 1501 Pope Alexander VI issued a special bull against the rebaptism of Orthodox in Poland,[79] and the papal delegate at the Synod of Vilna in 1521 tried to block rebaptism, but the local Synod of Piotrokow declared that the decision to have conditional rebaptism should be up to the convert, and the Synod of Przemysl (1554) insisted on conditional baptism. For the first time in the historical record, we see here that baptized Christians were insisting on a rite of passage to mark their transition into their new ecclesial community and perhaps

76. Yurij Zazuliak, "Rebaptism, Name-Giving and Identity among Nobles of Ruthenian Origin in Late Medieval Galicia," in *On the Frontier of Latin Europe: Integration and Segregation in Red Ruthenia, 1350-1600*, ed. Thomas Wünsch and Andrzej Janeczek (Warsaw: Institute of Archaeology and Ethnology of the Polish Academy of Sciences, University of Constance, 2004), 52; George Huntston Williams, *The Radical Reformation* (Philadelphia: Westminster Press, 1962), 1054n207.

77. Meyendorff, *Byzantium and the Rise of Russia*, 243n65.

78. Waclaw Hryniewicz, *The Challenge of Our Hope: Christian Faith in Dialogue* (Washington, DC: Council for Research in Values and Philosophy, 2007), 211.

79. Athanasius G. Welykyj, *Documenta Pontificum Romanorum Historiam Ucrainae Illustrantia (1075-1953)* (Rome: sump. Ucrainorum apud Exteros Degentium, 1953), vol. 1, 186–88, n. 108.

express their rejection of their previous baptism, a pastoral motivation that continues today.

It was not until the Council of Trent and its implementation in Poland by the Synod of Lvov (1564) that the rebaptism of Ruthenians was finally put to an end.[80] As in ninth-century Bulgaria, here we see central communities outlawing rebaptism, local clergy and now theologians defying these instructions as dissident enclaves, even though still in communion with the center. The aristocracy, rather than acting as cultural survivalists like Boris did, were in cahoots with the local clergy of their own ecclesial communion, a sign that the divisions between East and West were becoming more settled, more a matter of fact and identity than of two modes of Christian life.

The road toward a full break between Rome and Constantinople was thus actually quite long. The first signs of discordance began in the ninth century with the Photian schism, and perhaps originally the ostensibly crucial year of 1054 was also an ambiguous date.[81] In the Eastern Orthodox Church, a truly definitive moment came in 1484, when a synod of the four Eastern patriarchs at Constantinople affirmed

80. Hryniewicz, *Challenge of Our Hope*, 212–13. For more on Ruthenian rebaptism, see Edmund Przekop, "Die 'Rebaptizatio Ruthenorum' auf dem Gebiet Polens vor der Union von Brest (1596)," *Ostkirchliche Studien* 29 (1980): 273–82.

81. Kallistos (Timothy) Ware, "Orthodox and Catholics in the Seventeenth Century: Schism or Intercommunion?," in *Schism, Heresy and Religious Protest: Papers Read at the Tenth Meeting and the Eleventh Winter Meeting of the Ecclesiastical History Society*, ed. Derek Baker (Cambridge: Cambridge University Press, 1972), 259.

that Latin converts were to be received by anathema-chrismation.[82] This decision came in response to the failed Council of Florence (see pp. 78–79). There is no evidence in the historical record that this was a response to Western rebaptisms of Orthodox; rather, it seems to be the result of the crystallization of the understanding, among the Orthodox, of the growing theological differences between East and West (e.g., the issue of the *filioque* clause in the Creed).[83] In 1484, the patriarchs—at the highest level of ecclesial authority—finally formally declared the Western Church to be in a state of heresy; in fact, the decision followed a similar logic to that articulated by Mark of Ephesus, who had argued in the wake of Ferrara-Florence that Latins were much like Arians and should be received as such.[84]

82. That is, the patriarchs of the four ancient sees of the classical "pentarchy" which remained in communion with one another: Alexandria, Antioch, Constantinople, and Jerusalem; only Rome was excluded. See Ware, "Schism or Intercommunion?," 260. For the Greek text of the synodical decree, Council of Constantinople (1484), "Ὅρος τῆς ἁγίας καὶ οἰκουμενικῆς συνόδου ἥτις ἐπὶ ἀνατροπῇ συνέστητῆς ἐν Φλωρεντίᾳ," ed. S. Paschalidis, in *The Great Councils of the Orthodox Churches: Decisions and Synodika*, vol. 1, *From Constantinople 861 to Constantinople 1872*, ed. Alberto Melloni and Davide Dainese, CCCOGD 4/1 (Turnhout: Brepols, 2016), 225–28.

83. Ware, *Eustratios Argenti*, 63, notes that the five major issues between the two churches which were discussed at Florence did not include baptism, and only one involved ritual concerns: "The Council of Florence, in its *Decretum pro Graecis* (1439), singled out five issues which came later to be known in Eastern-Western polemics as the 'Five Differences': the Procession of the Holy Spirit; unleavened bread; purgatory; the blessedness of the Saints; and the Primacy of the Pope."

84. Cf. Ware, "Rebaptism of Heretics," 43.

Since Latin Christians were now understood as heretics, the synod of 1484 published a chrismation Office "for those who return from the Latin heresies to the orthodox and catholic Church."[85] Prior to this, only the aforementioned reception rite from the Great Church, first seen in *Barb. gr. 336* (ca. 787–800), had ever appeared in the liturgical books of Constantinople.[86] The new Office preserves some elements of the ancient rite, such as the renunciation and adherence ceremony prior to the chrismation, while also adapting the euchology of the chrism anointing to reflect a more penitential and less baptismal vision of Christian conversion.[87] Despite this, the chrismation service preserved the insistence of earlier Byzantine canonists and theologians on accepting trinitarian baptisms which had been celebrated outside of the church.

In conclusion, reception rites played a complex role in the relations between Eastern and Western Christians into the late Middle Ages. Against the opportunism of the periphery, the central authorities in both Rome and Constantinople consistently affirmed that the boundaries of the church's social body were permeable enough to permit "softer" reception rites, especially the use of written anathemas or professions of faith.

---

85. The Greek text can be found in Σύνταγμα τῶν θείων καὶ ἱερῶν κανόνων, ed. Georgios A. Ralles and Michael Potles (Athens: Chartophylakos, 1855), 5:143–47. An English translation is given by Dragas, "Manner of Reception," 238–41.

86. For the mss., see Miguel Arranz, "Les Sacrements de l'ancien Euchologe constantinopolitain (2): I'ère partie. Admission dans l'Église des convertis des hérésies ou d'autres religions non-chrétiennes," *Orientalia Christiana Periodica* 49 (1983): 42–90.

87. Calivas, "Receiving Converts," 184–87.

Only toward the end of the Middle Ages did theological polarization lead the Byzantine Orthodox Church to refine its position on ecclesial boundaries and insist on a stronger rite on the skin for the reception of Latin Christians. On the fringes of church authority, however, local actors often attempted to perceptibly strengthen those ecclesial boundaries by practicing rebaptism or applying obsolete rites of chrismation to new pastoral situations. Especially in the Latin West, distinctions between out-groups broke down as socio-ecclesial contexts evolved; rituals developed locally which treated all of those alienated from the church, for whatever reasons, with the same or even multiple rites on the skin. Consequently, these rites often seem to blur the boundaries between reception to the church, reconciliation with the church, and confirmation. It was this tension between centralized theological norms and local concerns which characterized the reception of baptized Christians on the cusp of the Protestant Reformation at the start of the early modern period.

# Chapter Five

# Settling into Schisms

Developments in the modern period before the dawn of the modern ecumenical movement crystallized the ongoing tension between theological affirmations (rebaptizing trinitarian heretics, not rebaptizing schismatics) and questions of practice (rebaptizing those who did not use a proper matter, form, and mode of baptism or chrismation) that were building in both East and West in earlier centuries. In the East, the questions raised by the reception of baptized Christians centered around a theological conflict between the "Cyprianic" assertion (named after Cyprian of Carthage) that there was no baptism outside the church and the principle from the Council of Nicaea (325) that baptisms in the name of the Trinity should not be repeated. In the realm of practice, these churches also debated the validity of the Western custom of baptizing without immersion and the validity of the consecration of chrism and hence the full initiation of Western churches. On their part, the Latin churches responded to the new schisms emerging in the Reformation by developing a new principle: the reception of baptized Christians was ritually determined not so much by their theological tradition of origin as by what rites they had received up to that point in the sequence of Christian initiation. This theological recentering of the reception of baptized Christians, depending more on initiation status than ecclesial belonging, was in some tension with the new rites, compiled from Western medieval source texts that did not conflate reception with confirmation.

## Early Modern Period
## (Sixteenth to Twentieth Centuries)

The 1484 synod in Constantinople ruled that Latin converts were to be received by chrismation and anathema, but as late as the seventeenth century, intercommunion (or *communicatio in sacris*) still existed in some places.[1] During this time, boundary practices between East and West varied widely. In the seventeenth century, conversions from the Greek to the Latin church did seem to occur but were largely performed through a "secret act of submission."[2] On the other hand, in Corfu there was clear intercommunion and Catholic

---

1. Kallistos (Timothy) Ware, "Orthodox and Catholics in the Seventeenth Century: Schism or Intercommunion?," in *Schism, Heresy and Religious Protest: Papers Read at the Tenth Meeting and the Eleventh Winter Meeting of the Ecclesiastical History Society*, ed. Derek Baker (Cambridge: Cambridge University Press, 1972), 262; Wilhelm de Vries, "Das Problem der 'communicatio in sacris cum dissidentibus' im Nahen Osten zur Zeit der Union (17. Und 18. Jahrhundert)," *Ostkirchliche Studien* 6 (1957): 81–106; Chrysostom Frank, "Orthodox-Catholic Relations," *Pro Ecclesia* 7, no. 1 (1998): 61–62.

2. Ware, "Orthodox and Catholics," 263.

priests even acknowledged the Orthodox bishop as their ordinary.[3] The 1484 synod's ruling was reaffirmed by synods in 1667 (Moscow), 1672 (Jerusalem), and ca. 1708 (Constantinople).[4] The latter synod extended the ruling to converts from the major Protestant communions, who prior to this seem to have been received by rebaptism. The central community of the Orthodox, then, demanded a middle approach to reception of Western baptized Christians, that is, a chrism rite on the skin that was not rebaptism. Nonetheless, in isolated local churches such as those on the Ionian islands, Latin converts were still received by rebaptism.[5] Thus in the East, as in the West, enclave-like communities that were

3. Frank, "Orthodox-Catholic Relations," 61–62; Ware, "Orthodox and Catholics," 262–63.

4. For English translations of the decrees of the synod of 1667, at which all the Eastern patriarchs were present, see "Extract from the MS. Acts of the Synod held at Moscow, A.D. 1666-1667, for the Deposition of the Patriarch Nicon," in *Dissertations on Subjects Relating to the "Orthodox" or "Eastern-Catholic" Communion* (London: Joseph Maters, 1853), 188–97. For the Russian texts, see E. V. Beljakova, "1666-7 Concilium Moscoviense," in *The Great Councils of the Orthodox Churches*, vol. 2, ed. Alberto Melloni, CCCOGD 4.2 (Turnhout: Brepols, 2017). For the decrees of the synod of 1672, a local synod which affirmed Western baptism, see Dositheos, *Confession* 15-16, in Ioannis Karmiris, Τα δογματικά καὶσυμβολικὰ μνημεῖα τῆς Ὀρθοδόξου Καθολικῆς Ἐκκλησίας, 2nd ed., vol. 2 (Graz, Austria: Akademische Druck- und Verlagsanstalt, 1968), 758–60. For the 1718 letter of Jeremiah III reporting on the synod of 1708, see Ioannis Karmiris, Τὰ δογματικὰ καὶ συμβολικὰ μνημεῖα τῆς Ὀρθοδόξου Καθολικῆς Ἐκκλησίας, 1st ed., vol. 2 (Athens: Apostoliki Diakoni, 1953), 1019.

5. Timothy (= Kallistos) Ware, *Eustratios Argenti: A Study of the Greek Church under Turkish Rule* (Oxford: Clarendon, 1964), 67–68.

still in communion with the central church defied its authority by mandating more extreme ritual actions on the skin of Christians being received.

Despite the unease of Byzantine canonists, theologians, and polemicists about Western baptismal methods (i.e., aspersion/affusion rather than three immersions), the influence of I Nicaea meant that trinitarian baptisms were not called into question again until the 1750s. Partially due to perceptions among the Orthodox that the Western Church had engaged in proselytism and other forms of anti-Orthodox aggression,[6] Patriarch Cyril V published an anathema against Latin baptism in 1755, and a 1756 synod under his presidency published a definition (Ὅρος) which declared Latin baptism null and void. These documents mention Latin deviations from the canons insisting on triple immersion,[7] but their main arguments seem to have been based theologically on a Cyprianic ecclesiology (see chapters 2 and 3). Revising their longstanding acceptance of trinitarian baptisms, the Byzantine Orthodox churches instituted a policy which held, in practice, that valid baptisms cannot be performed outside of the true church—in this case, the Eastern Orthodox Church.[8]

6. George D. Dragas, "The Manner of Reception of Roman Catholic Converts into the Orthodox Church with Special Reference to the Decisions of the Synods of 1484 (Constantinople), 1755 (Constantinople) and 1667 (Moscow)," *Greek Orthodox Theological Review* 44, no. 1–4 (1999): 243.

7. Ware, *Eustratios Argenti*, 86–100.

8. Kallistos Ware, "The Rebaptism of Heretics in the Orthodox Canonical Tradition," in *Heresy and the Making of European Culture: Medieval and Modern Perspectives*, ed. Andrew P. Roach

The 1756 definition signaled a rupture with the previous Byzantine approach to the reception of converts. By decreeing universal rebaptism, that is, it shunned the consistent tradition of accepting trinitarian water baptisms, even if their ritual form was not ideal; it also resurrected an ecclesiological position that was discreetly put to rest by I Nicaea can. 8's norm for accepting Novatians without rebaptism. The 1756 definition was later bolstered by Nikodemos the Hagiorite's publication in 1801 of a canonical manual called *The Rudder* (*Πηδάλιον*). In this manual, the Athonite canonist proposed an innovative hermeneutic aimed at resolving tensions in the canonical tradition. Misconstruing the origins of the "Apostolic Canons," which despite their name were actually composed in fourth-century Syria, Nikodemos had argued that baptism only exists within the canonical boundaries of the church.[9] He maintained that every historical relaxation of the strict requirement of universal baptism, even when articulated by the ecumenical councils, was a pastoral concession which compromised the strictness (ἀκρίβεια) of the church's dogma.[10] Subsequently, most decisions in Greek-speaking Orthodoxy which favored the reception of a convert by chrismation have

---

and James R. Simpson (London: Taylor and Francis, 2013), 45; Ware, *Eustratios Argenti*, 80–81.

9. David Heith-Stade, "Receiving Converts in the Orthodox Church: A Historical-Analytical Study of Eighteenth Century Greek Canon Law," *Ostkirchliche Studien* 59, no. 1 (2010): 108–10; Heith-Stade, "Receiving the Non-Orthodox: A Historical Study of Greek Orthodox Canon Law," *Studia Canonica* 44, no. 2 (2010): 422–25.

10. Heith-Stade, "Receiving Converts," 104–5.

been interpreted as an attenuation "by economy" (i.e., pastoral accommodation) of the canonical requirement to rebaptize every convert to Orthodoxy.[11]

This "Greek approach" to the reception of converts stands in contrast to the so-called "Russian approach" used by most of the Slavic Orthodox churches, which, influenced by Latin scholastic categories, focuses on whether a Christian's initiation is complete.[12] In 1667, a synod of the Eastern patriarchs in Moscow brought the Russian Church into line with the reception norm for Roman Catholics, anathema-chrismation, practiced in the rest of the Orthodox East.[13] From the time of Peter Moghila (1596–1647), the Orthodox theological schools in Eastern Europe were strongly influenced by Western scholasticism, so they evaluated baptisms on the basis of appropriate "matter" (water) and "form" (trinitarian invocation).[14] "Westernized" Russian thought also

11. This is especially true in light of an 1875 decision of the Ecumenical Patriarchate to broadly allow the reception of converts by chrism, but only as a pastorally expedient (i.e., "economic") derogation from the canonical requirement to rebaptize all of them. For the text (in English) and a discussion, see Dragas, "Manner of Reception," 247–48; see also Ware, "Rebaptism of Heretics," 48–49.

12. This terminology of a "Greek" approach and a "Russian" approach was developed by the Orthodox canonist John H. Erickson in his article "The Reception of Non-Orthodox into the Church: Contemporary Practice," *St. Vladimir's Theological Quarterly* 41 (1997): 4–10.

13. Prior to this, the Russian Church likely rebaptized all converts. For instance, earlier medieval documents (13th c.) reveal Western approbation of the practice, which a synod in Moscow in 1620 reaffirmed. See Dragas, "Manner of Reception," 251.

14. The following discussion follows, in part, Antoine Wenger, "La réconciliation des hérétiques dans l'Église russe. Le Trebnik de Pierre Moghila," *Revue des études byzantines* 12 (1954): 144–75.

held that Roman Catholics retained the apostolic succession despite the Great Schism. This meant that their bishops could validly consecrate chrism. Confirmed Catholics were seen as fully initiated Christians, albeit penitents who needed to return to the true fold of the Orthodox Church.[15] A 1757 synod thus decreed that Catholics are to be received in the Russian Church only by a confession of faith.[16]

The Russian approach, dating from the same 1757 synod, legislates that the reception of Protestant converts take place by anathema and chrismation, because they have not been fully initiated.[17] In contrast to its view of Catholics, Russian thought holds that the Protestant communions have not maintained apostolic succession. As such, Protestants cannot confect *myron* (= chrism); hence they must be received by the so-called "mystery of chrismation," anointed on all their senses.[18] This understanding of chrismation—as a second "sacrament" of initiation following baptism—is very different from the ancient Byzantine approach (see chapter 3 above), in which heretics were received to the church by an anointing with holy chrism which seems to have been conceived of as possessing reconciliatory and corrective characteristics. Finally, despite the clarity of the Byzantine approach, the reception

15. Nicholas E. Denysenko, *Chrismation: A Primer for Catholics* (Collegeville, MN: Liturgical Press, 2014), 46, 86–87.

16. Kamiel Duchatelez, "L'économie baptismale dans l'Église Orthodoxe," *Istina* 16 (1971): 34ff.

17. This synod solidified the decision taken in 1718, when the Patriarch of Constantinople sent a letter on the topic to Tsar Peter the Great. See Dragas, "Manner of Reception," 251; see also n. 4 above.

18. Erickson, "Reception of Non-Orthodox," 7.

services which appear in the various historical iterations of the Slavic *Trebnik* (= euchologion) or which are used in the modern jurisdiction represent various "conflations" of historical liturgical material.[19] Many of these focus on penitence rather than on accepting and "fixing" an extra-ecclesial trinitarian baptism.

In the West, the Jesuits sought to promote union with the Orthodox by restoring the Council of Florence beginning already in the 1570s. This council "in their view, remained still theoretically in force, although unjustifiably repudiated in practice by the Greeks."[20] Instead of reunion, their influence resulted in the Antiochene schism in 1724, ending the *communicatio in sacris*.[21] This is the schism that eventually led the Patriarchate of Constantinople—in 1756, as mentioned earlier—to require that Latin converts be received through rebaptism and not chrismation.[22] Some scholars have claimed that "neither side required the other to do penance as schismatics or heretics; nor was a formal act of reconciliation to the church required," but there is evidence of Western Christians being received by anathema and chrismation in some areas.[23]

19. Erickson, "Reception of Non-Orthodox," 10–13.

20. Ware, "Orthodox and Catholics," 264–69, here 265. See also Jerry Kloczowski, *A History of Polish Christianity* (New York: Cambridge University Press, 2000), 116–18.

21. Ware, "Orthodox and Catholics," 273; Frank, "Orthodox-Catholic Relations," 62.

22. Ware, "Orthodox and Catholics," 275. More on this below.

23. Frank, "Orthodox-Catholic Relations," 61; see also see Joseph G. Goodwine, *The Reception of Converts: Commentary with Historical Notes*, Canon Law Studies 198 (Washington, DC: The Catholic University of America Press, 1944), 120.

Turning to the West, the churches that arose as a result of the Reformation (Lutherans, Anglicans, etc.) were considered a serious threat to Roman Catholic ecclesial boundaries and were treated as heretical and schismatic groups. They, rather than the Eastern churches, became the primary focus of discussion. Of course, many of the first members of the Reformation churches had been validly initiated before any schism took place. Trent focused more on how each individual Christian was initially initiated and less on their ecclesial affiliation (at least in theory) when determining how to receive them into the Roman Catholic Church. While the traditional categories of "heretics, schismatics, and apostates" were still included in the ritual books, "validly baptized" and "confirmed" were the real categories determining how Christians were received. The Council of Trent reiterated the official position that baptism, confirmation, and holy orders were non-repeatable and that baptism could be administered outside the church, but it did not address the reception of baptized Christians.[24] As a result, the synod in Rouen in 1581 sought to apply the Tridentine principles about baptism to the reception of baptized Protestants, in particular those coming from the Calvinist tradition.[25] The discussion at the synod largely

24. Dale Sieverding, *The Reception of Baptized Christians: A History and Evaluation* (Chicago: Liturgy Training Publications, 2001), 25–26.

25. For the text from the Synod of Rouen, see Concilium Rothomagense, "Difficultas" 6, in *Sacrorum Conciliorum: Nova et Amplissima Collectio*, ed. Giovanni Domenico Mansi et al. (Venice: Antonius Zatta, 1758–1798; reprinted Paris: Hubert Welter, 1902), 34:671–72.

revolved around the validity of Protestant confirmation. They drew off of the PWD (see chapter 3 above), which had reconciled Arians, heretics, and apostates by the imposition of hand. The synod quickly split into three groups: 1) one that argued that the ceremonies lacking in baptism should be supplied, particularly with the imposition of hands, and understood this as confirmation; 2) another that argued that the ceremonies lacking in baptism should be supplied, again with the imposition of hands, and understood this as a form of reconciliation, not confirmation; and 3) a third group that sought a middle ground that did not require that all of the baptismal ceremonies that were lacking be supplied.[26] After reaching an impasse, the synod wrote to Rome. Gregory XIII (r. 1572–1585) determined that the ceremonies lacking in the convert's original baptism should be supplied; however, he left unanswered the larger question of whether Protestant confirmation is valid.[27] What was clear was that the reception of Protestants required more than a simple anathema; it required the reinscribing of the faith on the individual's body.

While Trent did not address the reception of Protestants into the Catholic Church, two documents after Trent did provide some clarity: the *Pontificale Roma-*

---

26. For more studies on this text, see Saint-Palais d'Aussac, *La Réconciliation des hérétiques dans l'Église Latine* (Paris: Aux Éditions franciscaines, 1943), 27–29; T. Mäder, "El sentido de la imposicion de la mano en el rito reconciliador de los penitentes y herejes en la práctica eclesiástica antigua del Occidente," *Ciencia y Fe* 18, no. 3–4 (1962): 317–19.

27. Sieverding, *Reception of Baptized Christians*, 26–27.

*num* of 1595[28] and the *Rituale Romanum* of 1614.[29] The adoption of the *Rituale Romanum* of 1614 was not universally required, but it exerted a strong influence on the Roman Catholic Church across the world. These new Tridentine liturgical books relied heavily on the earlier rituals for the reception of heretics, schismatics, and apostates in their ritual response to the emerging churches of the Reformation. The *Pontificale Romanum* of 1595 was largely a replication of the PWD. It contained a ritual for the reconciliation of schismatics, apostates, and heretics, which prescribed an imposition of hand and a pneumatic prayer.[30] There also remained some discrepancies with the way Easterners were received into the church.[31]

28. See p. 86, n. 49 above.

29. For the edition of the latter, see *Rituale Romanum. Editio Princeps (1614)*, ed. Manlio Sodi and Juan Javier Flores Arcas, Monumenta Liturgica Concilii Tridentini 5 (Vatican City: Libreria Editrice Vaticana, 2004).

30. Sieverding, *Reception of Baptized Christians*, 27–28.

31. In this complex period of time there were three ways in which the Roman Catholic Church approached the Orthodox and even Oriental churches: (1) Latinization; (2) Uniate churches; and (3) personal adherence. For an overview, see Ines Angjeli Murzaku, *Returning Home to Rome: The Basilian Monks of Grottaferrata in Albania* (Roma: Monastero esarchico, Grottaferrata, 2009), 15–19. In all cases but the last, no ritual seems to have been necessary, and even the last case does not always seem to require one. For more on the formation of the Uniate churches, see Ernst Christoph Suttner, *Church Unity: Union or Uniatism?: Catholic-Orthodox Ecumenical Perspectives* (Rome/Bangalore: Centre for Indian and Inter-Religious Studies/ Dharmaram Publications, 1991). Clearly these uniate churches provide yet another wrinkle in our history, since whole churches, through the consent of the bishop, were brought into union with Rome apparently without any formal liturgical ritual.

The *Rituale Romanum* of 1614 provided some further guidance in the *praenotanda*, which outlined three possible ways for receiving adults baptized outside of the Catholic Church: 1) if the validity of their baptism was doubtful, they were to be conditionally baptized; 2) if their baptism was invalid, they were to be baptized; and 3) if they were properly baptized, the rest of the ceremonies lacking in their baptism should be added, but the ordinary could decide to dispense them.[32] This included chrismation for adults and infants and the administration of confirmation for those who had not received it, though again these ceremonies could be dispensed with. This is further affirmed by the rubric about confirmation ("if they are to be confirmed"), which seems to indicate that confirmation did not always follow.[33] This suggests a distinction between the administration of confirmation and the rite of reception. Thus, a distinction was made between supplying the rites they missed at baptism as the mode of receiving them, and then later confirming them. Even those Catholics who were baptized in an emergency were supposed to have these rituals supplied—and confirmation would have been a separate ritual from the process of supplying the rituals absent in their baptism.

While the *Rituale Romanum* seemed to provide clarity to the ritual process, it also diverged to some degree from the *Pontificale Romanum*, so it is unclear

32. Cf. Sieverding, *Reception of Baptized Christians*, 28–29; Paul Turner, *When Other Christians Become Catholic* (Collegeville, MN: Liturgical Press, 2007), 39–40.

33. If it did follow the rite of reception, those being received experienced a double chrismation: post-baptismal chrismation—imposition of hand—confirmation with chrismation.

how exactly the reception of baptized Christians was administered. Likely it depended on the region and time period. This could mean that, on the one hand, Orthodox Christians and Protestants who were baptized as Catholics (and who were thus apostates) would have fallen under the ritual of the 1595 *Pontificale.* On the other hand, the expanded renunciation of false worship included in the full baptismal liturgy in the 1614 *Rituale* may have been appropriate for those who converted from paganism, Judaism, or Islam, as well as for those who were baptized as Protestants (e.g., heretics and sects of the impious), the validity of whose previous baptism was thus in question, and so were conditionally baptized.

Thus, both the *Pontificale Romanum* and the *Rituale Romanum* left the more significant question about the validity of Protestant confirmation largely unanswered. Furthermore, here, for the first time, it was technically the administration of the rites themselves rather than ecclesial belonging that established the ritual that was to be used. However, in practice in many places, and in the East as well, it was still ecclesial belonging that motivated how these directives were implemented. While for Protestants all that was technically needed if their baptism was valid was an absolution from excommunication, Turner notes that conditional baptism seems to have been the norm: "In practice priests baptized conditionally almost everyone who had been previously baptized in a church considered heretical."[34] While this was, as in Bulgaria and

---

34. Turner, *When Other Christians Become Catholic,* 40. Sieverding notes that all that was necessary for Protestants was an absolution from excommunication, but especially in the United States conditional

Ukraine, a contradiction with central, official church teaching, it served as a rite on the skin that would highlight the boundary between other ecclesial communities and the Catholic Church.

In the United States, in the First National Synod of 1791, conditional rebaptism was upheld, as was the need to supply the necessary ceremonies.[35] These discrepancies likely explain why a clarification on the manner for the reception of baptized Christians was issued by the Holy Office in 1859 in response to a question posed by the archbishop of Philadelphia:

> In the conversion of heretics, the first inquiry needs to be about the validity of the baptism received in heresy. Therefore, after a diligent examination has been made, if it is found that no baptism was conferred, or that it was conferred invalidly, they are to be baptized absolutely. If, when the investigation is completed, the validity of the baptism is still in doubt, baptism must be given conditionally (*sub-conditione*). Finally, if it is established that the baptism received was valid, they are to be received only with the abjuration or profession of faith . . . 1) if the baptism is conferred absolutely, no abjuration or absolution follows, as all has been washed away in the sacrament of regeneration. 2) If baptism is repeated condition-

baptism became standard practice; see Sieverding, *Reception of Baptized Christians*, 30. Much more work is needed on what the standard practice was, especially outside of the United States and England.

35. Sieverding, *Reception of Baptized Christians*, 35–36. For the text of the council, see *Concilia Provincialia, Baltimori: ab anno 1829 usque ad annum 1849* (Baltimore: Joannem Murphy et Socium, 1851), 12–13.

ally, this is the order: a) abjuration or profession of faith b) conditional baptism c) sacramental confession with conditional absolution. 3) When the baptism is judged to be valid, abjuration or profession of faith alone and the absolution from censures follows.[36]

Notably the imposition of hands is not referenced, nor is the supplying of the baptismal ceremonies. The abjuration of heresy and profession of faith was quite long and apologetic, though a shorter form was allowed for "the uneducated and for those who do not have the religious development to understand the longer formula."[37] A similar statement in 1878 on rebaptism does not mention the liturgical ritual either, nor does it mention the imposition of hands.[38] An a-ritual reception appears to have become the norm in places like United States, at least in theory,[39] and oftentimes ordinaries in England and the United States dispensed from the extra ceremonies.[40] Orthodox and Oriental Christians appear to have been received by the bishop through an abjuration of heresy and a profession of

36. Sieverding, *Reception of Baptized Christians*, 34. For the text, see *Instructio S. Congreg. S. Officii, de neoconversorum receptione (20 July 1859)*, in *Codicis Iuris Canonici Fontes*, vol. 4, *Curia Romana* (Vatican City: Vatican, 1951), 226–29.

37. *Collectio Rituum* (Collegeville, MN: Liturgical Press, 1964), 193–95.

38. *Codicis Iuris Canonici Fontes*, 4:380.

39. Sieverding, *Reception of Baptized Christians*, 34–38; Turner, *When Other Christians Become Catholic*, 41–43.

40. Adrian Fortescue and J. B. O'Connell, *The Ceremonies of the Roman Rite Described* (Westminster, MD: Newman Press, 1962), 365–69 and 411–14.

faith.[41] Mention is also made of the validity of their baptism and confirmation.[42]

## Historical and Ritual Conclusions

The reception of baptized Christians has troubled ecumenical relationships throughout Christian history. The tension we originally described between the theological recognition of other churches' initiatory practices and the pastoral care of individuals is complicated by communities' need for well-defined identity. Even today, there are parishes, ministers, and also candidates for full communion who would prefer to shore up denominational identity by performing more elaborate rites for Christians than are actually required, and we can see in this conflict a reflection of what happened in ninth-century Bulgaria and fifteenth-century Poland, as well as a reflection of the practices of many nineteenth-century Orthodox priests. While there is a high degree of variation in the way in which baptized Christians

41. T. Lincoln Bouscaren, *The Canon Law Digest: Officially Published Documents Affecting the Code of Canon Law 1917–1933* (Milwaukee: Bruce Publishing, 1934), 849–53. Goodwine notes how Oriental Christians were received: "Since it is generally recognized that the baptisms conferred by Oriental dissidents are valid, the usual procedure in the reception of an oriental convert will embrace the abjuration of former errors, the profession of faith and the absolution from the censure of excommunication, if the case warrants it." Here he includes a footnote that also references the "Greek schismatics" alongside the "Oriental heretics," suggesting this is similar to the manner of receiving them. Goodwine, *Reception of Converts*, 166.

42. Bouscaren, *Canon Law Digest*, 851.

have been received in the East and West, it is worth highlighting some key insights from the history.

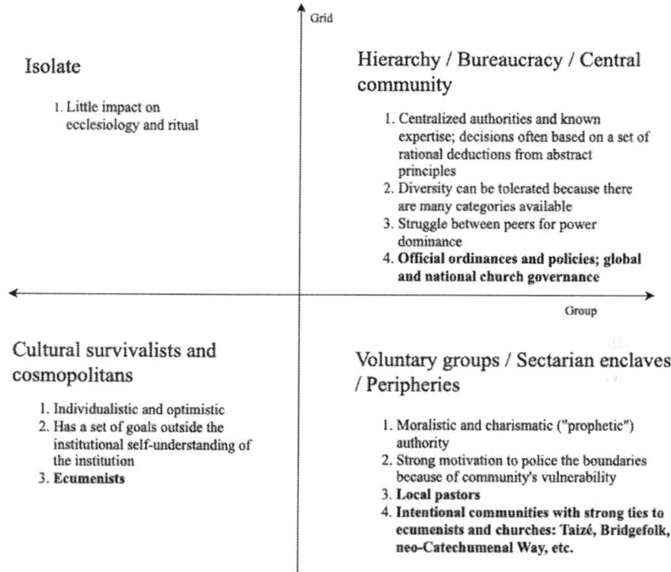



**Figure 5.1.** One possible categorization of some of the active groups in ecumenical relationships today. There are both pro- and anti-ecumenical voluntary groups; the pro-ecumenical groups obviously cross ecclesial boundary lines.

By the third century, the reception of individuals baptized outside of the church was already an issue that affected the whole church. Discussions were particularly shaped by the differing concerns of two of the main centers of Latin-speaking Christianity: the church in Rome on the one hand, and the church in Carthage in North Africa on the other. In the late patristic and early medieval periods, the reception of baptized

Christians was increasingly an issue confined to what we have referred to as the "ecclesial borderlands," such as the western (Iberia) and eastern (Balkans) peripheries of the Western Church.

In this period, while the use of chrism was maintained in some ritual texts into the Middle Ages, the early Roman tradition of imposing hands largely won out in the West, theologically interpreted in various ways. It was perceived sometimes as an act of reconciliation or connected to initiation, but at other times as a combination of the two—that is, as a ritual act which both reconciles the convert and completes his or her initiation. Despite this confusion, the laying on of hands can be taken as *the* historical act of reception in the churches of Western Christianity.

In the churches of the West, baptism has usually been perceived as being connected to larger social realities and structures. This includes not only larger ecclesial structures, such as episcopal or synodal—or even papal—authority, but also political structures like monarchs and national churches. Individuals are often treated distinctly from whole churches and clergy, whose reception is perceived as having larger ecclesial (not to mention social) implications. More research is needed on both the historical development and ritual understanding of reception at this larger level.

Instances of rebaptism in the Western Church have often been the result of local divergences from official Roman policy, motivated by political realities or social perceptions. However, one can also question how experientially and ritually distinct the so-called "conditional baptism" was from rebaptism. This practice was generally applied even to those with supposedly "valid" baptisms. It was prominent in the pre-Tridentine period, and was given further support in the post-Tridentine liturgical books for all those separated from the Roman Catholic Church by "heresy" or "schism." Conditional baptism remained widely practiced—with official justification —into the middle of the twentieth century.

In fact, since the synod of Rouen in 1581, the Roman Catholic Church has struggled to determine how to theologically understand the reception of baptized Christians from the churches of the Reformation. This seems to be motivated by the questions about the ecclesial status of their confession of origin (heresy? schism?) as well as confusion about their initial initiation (do the Protestant communities have valid confirmation?). From the time of the liturgical reforms following the Council of Trent, this situation was especially complicated given the practice of "supplying the rites" missing in baptism. Even Christians whose baptisms were treated as valid—and who were thus not conditionally baptized—were still made to undergo all the other usual rites of Roman baptism upon their entry to the church: exorcism, the use of salt and saliva, the various anointings, etc.

Some of this confusion—but certainly not all—was resolved after the Second Vatican Council with the publication of a rite of reception for baptized Christians in the *Order of Christian Initiation of Adults* (OCIA), previously known in most English-speaking circles as the *Rite of Christian Initiation of Adults* (RCIA). In this rite (currently in use), baptized Christians from the churches of the Reformation are normally received by confirmation, even though technically the laying on of hands should suffice. That is, while on an official level the question of Protestant confirmation has never been resolved, in normative practice Protestant converts are treated as "not fully initiated," lacking the sacrament of confirmation, and thus they are received into the Catholic Church by confirmation. In the Roman Catholic Church, in short, the theology and ritual practice of the reception of baptized Christians has never been fully settled (see chapter 6 below).

Turning our gaze again to the East, it should be stressed that since the fourth century, the authoritative synods—starting with I Nicaea (325)—have ordered the acceptance of some converts' baptisms. By the 360s, the local council of Laodicea had instituted the reception of Novatians, Photinians, and Quartodecimans by the anointing with chrism. The fifth-century practice of Constantinople was to receive validly baptized Christians with an anointing with chrism—with the baptismal formula "Seal of the gift of the holy Spirit"—after an anathema of errors. The spurious Canon 7 of I Constantinople (610–641) and the authentic Canon 95 of the Council of Trullo (691–692) extended this practice to the whole Byzantine Church. From the fifth century, members of groups that dissent from the fifth-century councils of Ephesus and Chalcedon have been received by a formal anathema. This would also be codified for the whole Byzantine Church by Trullo can. 95. The "official" tradition of interpreting these canons begins with and depends on Basil of Caesarea's *First Canonical Letter*, which affirmed that those baptized into the Trinity outside of the church are to be received by the anointing with chrism; those belonging to non-trinitarian groups are to be rebaptized.

Theologically speaking, the anointing of baptized converts with chrism was sometimes justified as an action which "heals" the convert of their heresy. A number of theologians also mentioned the necessity of a chrism-anointing because some "heretical" groups do not use chrism in their initiation. The Byzantine liturgy of reception in *Barberini gr. 336* emphasizes the reconciliation with and perfection of an erring Christ-follower in the church. Apart from the baptismal anointing formulas, it does not reference initiation in its orations. Conversely, the liturgy for receiving Roman Catholic converts (1484) turns toward themes of penitence rather than healing and reconciliation. It also does not repeat the idea of a "completed initiation," despite the use of the post-baptismal chrismation formula.

Because several canons mention the Byzantine practice of baptism normatively occurring by three immersions, by the eleventh century some pastors seem to be justifying the practice of rebaptizing Western Christians—when Western baptism had come to acquire the form of pouring or sprinkling (i.e., non-immersive methods). Sociopolitical factors seem to have influenced this (usually) nonofficial application of these canons. This seems to have followed periods of Western provocation—such as the Crusades, the growth of Rome's *Propaganda Fide* in the sixteenth century, and Jesuit-backed schisms in the early eighteenth century. From the middle of the eighteenth century, polemical literature takes the "Cyprianic" position that Western Christians are "outside" the true church and thus do not possess real baptism. This is especially reflected in the 1801 canonical manual *The Rudder* (Πηδάλιον) of Nikodemos the Hagiorite. In Russia, theology is influenced by Western scholasticism, so that from the seventeenth century Protestants have been received by anointing with chrism (because the Protestant churches are not believed to possess apostolic succession, and thus have no confirmation), while confirmed Catholics are received by confession and anathema (because their confirmation is acknowledged).

Currently, Western Christians are received by chrism (usually with a penitential twist) in the Greek churches—as a pastoral attenuation of the need to rebaptize—while in the Russian churches, the scholastic approach generally prevails. The liturgical services used today are an ahistorical conglomeration of themes of penitence and the completion of initiation. These conclusions reflect the practice and theory of the ancient Byzantine Church and its historical descendants among the Eastern Orthodox Churches.

## Interlude: Other Eastern Churches

Further scholarly work is sorely needed with regards to the reception of converts in the non-Byzantine East. In the Coptic Church some early sources point to simply the reception of communion as the way at least to become part of the Chalcedonian church; however, a written anathema was often required.[43] Also, it is interesting that conversion between the Chalcedonian and non-Chalcedonian churches was frequent at pilgrimage centers, where the efficacy of the healing was tied to "correct" religious belonging.[44] The situation of clergy,

43. Béatrice Caseau, "Ordinary Objects in Christian Healing Sanctuaries," in *Objects in Context, Objects in Use: Material Spatiality in Late Antiquity*, ed. Luke Lavan, Ellen Swift, and Toon Putzeys, Late Antique Archaeology 5 (Leiden: Brill, 2007), 642 and 646–47.

44. Ewa Wipszycka, *The Alexandrian Church: People and Institutions* (Warsaw: Journal of Juristic Papyrology, 2015), 292–93.

however, was different, and this was especially an issue in Egypt where there were two churches.[45] In the medieval period, the Coptic Church developed the "Rite of the Jar" primarily for those who had apostatized and returned to the church.[46] The rite has essentially two parts. The first is the pouring of water over the penitent in a trinitarian formula that begins "I wash N. in the name of the . . ." The second part involves the anointing of the upper part of the body with blessed oil. The rite is in need of further investigation: it mirrors baptism, while very clearly attempting to not be a rebaptism. The rite existed at least in 1374, as Ugo Zanetti has recently argued based on the manuscripts, and also made its way into the Ethiopian Rite.[47] The *Canons of Clement* (also known as the *Canons of Peter* or the *Letter of Peter*), dated to Egypt between 850 and 1060, may preserve earlier evidence of the "Rite of the Jar." It suggests that those who have apostatized can be received back in a second baptism (§30).[48]

The Syrian situation, especially in the Oriental Orthodox Churches, is much more complex and not homogenous. One of the first distinctly Syrian references

45. Wipszycka, *Alexandrian Church*, 136–37 and 285–98.

46. For an English translation, see Raphael Tuki, *Pontificale et euchologium Alexandrium* (1761), 462–75; O. H. E. Khs-Burmester, *The Egyptian or Coptic Church* (Cairo: Publications De La Société D'archéologie Copte, 1967), 316–20.

47. Ugo Zanetti, "Bohairic Liturgical Manuscripts," *Orientalia Christiana Periodica* 61 (1995): 82.

48. Wilhelm Riedel, *Die Kirchenrechtsquellen des Patriarchats Alexandrien* (Leipzig: A. Deichert, 1900), 173; Johannes Hofmann, *Unser heiliger Vater Klemens: ein römischer Bischof im Kalender der griechischen Kirche*, Trierer theologische Studien 54 (Trier: Paulinus-Verlag, 1992), 36–39.

for how to treat apostates coming from a different tradition appears in Canon 19 of an East Syrian synod held in 554. The ritual requires an anointing with the "oil of prayer," which is sometimes identified with the oil used in the pre-baptismal rites.[49] For those who have apostatized or for some heretics being received into the church, the East Syrian Church follows the "Rite of Forgiveness," which uses the same oil used in baptism, thus mirroring the East Syrian synod of 554.[50] The Syrian Orthodox Church's history of reception is more complex,[51] and at times it appears that the reception uses an anointing similar to, or even the same as, the anointing of the sick in the Syrian Orthodox Church's "Rite of the Candle."[52] The Melkites appear to have baptized those coming from the heresy of Mani and Arius, and simply accepted an abjuration of heresy from the Jacobites, Nestorians, Maronites, and Armenians. Anointing was no longer used in the Melkite tradition except for those who had converted

49. J.-B. Chabot, *Synodicon Orientale* (Paris, 1902), 363–64; Sebastian Brock, "The Syriac Tradition," in *The Oil of Gladness: Anointing in the Christian Tradition*, ed. Martin Dudley and Geoffrey Rowell (London/Collegeville, MN: SPCK/Liturgical Press, 1993), 97n19.

50. Brock, "Syriac Tradition," 97. For the "Rite of Forgiveness," see J. Isaac, *Ṭaksa d-Ḥussaya: Le rite du pardon dans l'Eglise syriaque orientale*, Orientalia Christiana Analecta 233 (Rome: Pontifical Oriental Institute, 1989), 68–69 and 112–13.

51. Wilhelm de Vries, *Sakramententheologie bei den syrischen Monophysiten*, Orientalia Christiana Analecta 125 (Rome: Pontifical Oriental Institute, 1940), especially 17–89.

52. Brock, "Syriac Tradition," 97. For the "Rite of the Candle," see de Vries, *Sakramententheologie bei den syrischen Monophysiten*, 211–21.

to Islam and returned, which shifted the ritual practice for receiving Arians.[53] Further work is needed on the West Syrian rites for the reception of apostates and heretics, which remains quite diverse across the various West Syrian communities.

The reception of those baptized in other churches entering into the Armenian Church has also not been studied by scholars.[54] A possible source for further information on the reception of baptized Christians into the Armenian Church may appear in the work of Mkhitar the Thinbearded (1130–1213), who discusses the relationship between the Armenians and Georgians. The current Armenian Church does not have a specific ritual for reconciling heretics or receiving back apostates; however, there is a ritual of renunciation and creedal affirmation at the beginning of the Armenian prayerbook that was used for Armenian Catholics returning to the Armenian Church.[55] Today it is used for restoring priests to holy orders, but its use as a rite of reception today is not clear.

53. See Sinai, Syr. MS 42 ff. 68v-69r, dated to the 12th cent.; Sinai, Syr. 109 f. 82r, dated to 1221; Vatican, Borgia Syr. 13 f. 116v, dated to 13th cent.; and Paris Syr. 100 f. 30v, dated to the 16th cent. For more, we referred to the unpublished paper by Paul Elhallal, "The Melkite Rites for Reconciling Heretics." We are grateful for his help.

54. The information on the Armenian Church included here is taken from a personal communication with Gregoris Shokhikyan (February 7, 2023). We are grateful for his help. See also Gregory Shokhikyan, "The Church of Armenia and the Sacramental Sharing: Historical Horizon, Future Perspectives," *Review of Ecumenical Studies Sibiu* 14, no. 1 (April 1, 2022): 100–122.

55. For the creed, see D. D. Dowling, *The Armenian Church* (London: SPCK, 1910), 64–66.

Chapter Six

# Ecumenical Revisions

## *The Twentieth Century, Today, and the Future*

Because of the liturgical movement and the ecumenical movement, twentieth-century changes to the rites of reception were influenced by historical research into liturgy and by developing ecumenical commitments. In the Orthodox churches, distinct Russian and Greek approaches, with their different ecclesiological and pastoral implications, have crystallized, leaving behind the question of whether there is salvation outside the Orthodox communion. In the West, robust ecumenical commitments have developed, but they are sometimes in pastoral tension with the practice of reception of baptized Christians. The liturgical reforms identified reception with confirmation (something not obvious from the documentary history in the West) and strongly asserted the early church order of the sacraments of initiation: baptism, confirmation, Eucharist. The reformed rites further shifted the interpretation of confirmation closer to Eastern chrismation, even adopting the Eastern formula invoking the Holy Spirit. The result was a reduction of the complex theological meanings (ecclesial belonging, episcopal communion, penitence, orthodox faith, initiation, healing) of reception into a theology dominated by initiation, especially when performed alongside baptisms at the Easter Vigil. While this has caused ecumenical challenges, the resulting theological interpretation of reception as an acknowledgement and renewal of trinitarian baptism has been ecumenically received through much of Western Christianity and is a promising step. In this chapter, we will describe the process of liturgical renewal in the Roman Catholic Church and draw conclusions for ecumenical best practices and recommend further reforms.

## East

A coherent liturgical ecclesiology, such as that which existed in the Byzantine Church before the fall of Constantinople in 1453, can seem to be lacking in contemporary Orthodoxy. Dispute over ecclesiological basics is evident when the same Christian convert—in this case, a Roman Catholic—previously baptized into the Holy Trinity, can be received by rebaptism in the Russian Orthodox Church Outside of Russia (ROCOR),[1] chrismation in the Greek and Antiochian

---

1. This is justified on the basis of a twentieth-century Russian theory of economy. For a historical overview of the theory, see Andrei V. Psarev, "The 19th Canonical Answer of Timothy of Alexandria: On the History of Sacramental Oikonomia," *St. Vladimir's Theological Quarterly* 51, no. 2–3 (2007): 297–320; for the ROCOR decree on rebaptism, still in effect, see Synod of the Russian Orthodox Church Outside of Russia, "Decree on the Question of the Baptism of Heretics (15/28 September 1971)," *Orthodox Life* 29, no. 2 (1979): 35–36.

Orthodox archdioceses in North America, and confession and communion in the Orthodox Church in America (OCA).[2] Just as in the rebaptism controversies of ancient North Africa, this diversity of practice reflects contradictory understandings of baptism and church membership, as well as a dispute over the existence of Christian faith and sacraments outside of the canonical boundaries of the Eastern churches.[3] Similarly, the different uses of chrism—the Greek versus the Russian approaches—suggest variant ecclesiology. Currently, Western Christians are received by chrism in the Greek churches, understood as a pastoral attenuation of the strict canonical requirement to rebaptize. In many churches of the Russian tradition, such as the Patriarchate of Moscow and the OCA (though not the ROCOR), the scholastic approach normatively prevails, in that Protestants are chrismated while

2. See the Orthodox Church in America's *Service for the Reception of Converts* (Yonkers, NY: St. Vladimir's Seminary Press, 1989); John H. Erickson, "The Reception of Non-Orthodox into the Church: Contemporary Practice," *St. Vladimir's Theological Quarterly* 41 (1997): 11–13.

3. See Akliviadis C. Calivas, "Receiving Converts into the Orthodox Church: Lessons from the Canonical and Liturgical Tradition," in *The Liturgy in Dialogue: Exploring and Renewing the Tradition*, Essays in Liturgy and Theology 5 (Brookline, MA: Holy Cross Orthodox Press, 2018), 141–44; John Klentos, "Rebaptizing Converts into the Orthodox Church: Old Perspectives on a New Problem," *Studia Liturgica* 29 (1999): 216–17. For the question on the relationship between the church's canonical boundaries and sacramental grace, see the classic article by Georges Florovsky, "The Boundaries of the Church," in *Collected Works of Georges Florovsky*, vol. 13, *Ecumenism I: A Doctrinal Approach*, ed. Richard S. Haugh (Belmont, MA: Nordland, 1989), 36–45 [= "The Limits of the Church," *Sourozh* 26 (1986, translation of 1933 original): 13–24].

(confirmed) Catholics are not. The ecumenical implications of this discord are obvious. Broadly construed, the Russian approach suggests a positive appreciation of the relationship of non-Orthodox Christians to the church. It also acknowledges the existence of some sacraments in non-Orthodox communions. But the Greek approach implies a negative attitude toward non-Orthodox Christians. On the one hand, it claims that the sacraments of other Christian communions do not share in God's grace. This implies that these communities, even though professing faith in Christ, can hardly be called Christian. On the other hand, the Greek approach even suggests that the Orthodox Church possesses authority over the sacraments, including those of other communions.

## West

On the other hand, the Roman Catholic Church in the twentieth century developed, for the first time, rites specifically for the "reception of baptized Christians," terminology that was developed and adopted in this period. This rite, the result of the liturgical reforms of the Second Vatican Council, emphasized the importance of the valid baptism of candidates for full communion. The rite that emerged finally broke with many of the categorical distinctions that no longer seemed relevant, eliminating entirely the language of heretics, schismatics, and apostates in conformity with the conciliar documents. The rite that was developed relied on scholarship on how baptized Christians had historically been received: the rites for the reception of heretics, schismatics, and apostates (see chapter 4 above), as well as the Tridentine practice of supplementing the rites that had been omitted in their original baptism (see chapter 5 above). At the same time, the new rite was also influenced by developing ecumenical partnerships and by a concern to sacramentally educate Catholics on the importance of the ancient initiatory pattern in which baptism was immediately followed by chrismation and communion. The new rite was meant to distinguish between individuals coming from the Eastern and Reformation churches, as well as distinguishing both from catechumens for baptism.

The new rite for the reception of Eastern Christians was in continuity with the historical tradition: a simple profession of faith was all that was required before admission to communion. This had been formalized in the conciliar document *Orientalium Ecclesiarum* (1964)[4] and reflected in the first Ecumenical Directory (*Ad totam ecclesiam*, 1967), which validated the baptism and "confirmation" of Eastern Christians.[5] *Ad*

4. *Orientalium Ecclesiarum* 25. The conciliar text was published in *Acta Apostolica Sedis* 57 (1965): 76–85. For a discussion, see Dale Sieverding, *The Reception of Baptized Christians: A History and Evaluation* (Chicago: Liturgy Training Publications, 2001), 54.

5. *Ad totam ecclesiam* 12. The first Ecumenical Directory was published in *Acta Apostolica Sedis* 59 (1967): 574–92. "There can be no doubt cast upon the validity of baptism as conferred upon separated Eastern Christians. It is enough therefore to establish the fact that baptism was administered. Since in the Eastern Churches the sacrament of confirmation (chrism) is always lawfully administered by the priest at the same time as baptism, it often happens that no mention is made of the confirmation in the canonical testimony of baptism. This does not give grounds for doubting that the sacrament was conferred." English translation quoted in Sieverding, *Reception of Baptized Christians*, 56–57. The Ecumenical Directory's conflation of chrismation and confirmation, while intended to prevent repetition of the former, could be given more nuance.

*totam ecclesiam* also limits conditional baptism for individuals coming from the churches of the Reformation to situations where the validity of baptism is seriously questioned.[6] Referencing the conciliar Decree on Ecumenism, *Ad totam ecclesiam* distinguished those "born and baptized outside the visible communion of the Catholic Church" from those who "though baptized in the Catholic Church, have knowingly and publically abjured her faith."[7] This clarified that those received from Reformation churches were not schismatics or apostates; these terms are reserved for Catholics who have openly broken their ties with the church.

Those baptized outside of the visible communion of the Catholic Church were not judged responsible for ecclesial schisms. "In the absence of such blame," the Directory noted, "if they freely wish to embrace the Catholic faith, they have no need to be absolved from excommunication, but after making profession of their faith according to the regulations set down by the ordinary of the place they should be admitted to the full communion of the Catholic Church."[8] In addition, then, to omitting any hint of grave sin (and thus sacramental penance), the Directory implies that only an act of reception would be required for establishing full communion, not

6. *Ad totam ecclesiam* 14–15. See *Acta Apostolica Sedis* 59 (1967): 574–92.

7. *Ad totam ecclesiam* 19. See *Acta Apostolica Sedis* 59 (1967): 574–92. English translation quoted in Sieverding, *Reception of Baptized Christians*, 57.

8. *Ad totam ecclesiam* 19. See *Acta Apostolica Sedis* 59 (1967): 574–92. English translation quoted in Sieverding, *Reception of Baptized Christians*, 57.

the sacrament of confirmation.[9] The *Consilium* tasked with the reform of the Roman liturgy, however, took the rite of reception in a different direction.

The shaping of the new *ordo* for the rite of reception took as its starting point the conceptual paradigm that sees admission to the church as the final step or "completion" of the process of Christian initiation. In this framework, initiation starts with baptism and is brought to its fulfillment by confirmation and reception of the Eucharist. As Paul Turner says, "The opinion that confirmation must precede Eucharist would seem obvious to the Eastern Churches. Yet it has little foundation in the liturgical practice of the West."[10] Frederick McManus (1923–2005), a canonist and liturgical expert who participated in the reform of this *ordo*, summarized this part of the discussion:

> [T]he order of admission completes the initiation begun in baptism; indeed if possible, it should be linked with the conferral of confirmation and eucharistic participation. If the one admitted is from the Orthodox (who already have valid sacraments of initiation), mention should be made of the initiation already completed as the foundation of admission.[11]

9. *Ad totam ecclesiam* 19–20. See *Acta Apostolica Sedis 59* (1967): 574–92. English translation quoted in Sieverding, *Reception of Baptized Christians*, 57.

10. Paul Turner, *When Other Christians Become Catholic* (Collegeville, MN: Liturgical Press, 2007), 60.

11. This is from a letter of McManus to a Father Hotckin, 1 August 1967, quoted in Sieverding, *Reception of Baptized Christians*, 66 and 137.

The paradigm baptism-confirmation-Eucharist was taken from early church sources that were broadly accepted by both East and West, but the rites are now used to address ecclesial relationships and conditions that did not exist in the early church. Most urgently, these include the existence of large, stable ecclesial communities in partial communion with Rome (see *Unitatis Redintegratio* [UR] 3, 22; *Ut Unum Sint* 11) who do not practice post-baptismal, episcopal chrismation. The rite also reflects an ongoing tension between confirmation practiced before communion in Eastern Catholic churches and in some Latin Catholic dioceses—that is, in dioceses with a "restored order" of initiation, or which celebrate confirmation at the Easter Vigil or in emergency situations—and confirmation practiced as an adolescent rite of passage after First Communion or in adulthood.

As the foundation of the *Order of Christian Initiation of Adults* (OCIA), of course, the "restored order" of the sacraments of baptism, confirmation, and Eucharist was based on the ancient catechumenate, but it also created a psychologically and ritually satisfying experience of integration into the church for many catechumens. As the basis for an *ordo* of reception, however, the sacramental progression of baptism, confirmation, and Eucharist represented a radical departure from significant parts of the tradition. While the medieval Western rites of reception certainly drew on orations similar to that of confirmation in their evocation of the sevenfold gifts of the Spirit (see chapter 3), the sacrament of confirmation had never been seen as a necessary ritual for entry to the church, largely because so few lay faithful received it through much of the Middle Ages. Additionally, while elements of the initiation rites were sometimes incorporated into the rite of reception—such as the *ordo* in William Durandus's pontifical (PWD, see chapter 4 above)—such liturgical ceremonies were never understood to "complete" initiation. But the several schemas for a reformed *ordo*, which were composed and refined by the *Consilium* from 1967 to 1968, nevertheless centered on the relationship between profession, imposition, and confirmation.

This notion of a completed initiation would likely have been foreign to the compilers of the Tridentine *Rituale Romanum*, and it was also disputed in the *Consilium* itself. In its *praenotanda*, the *Rituale Romanum* (1614) implied a liturgical distinction between the act of reception and the sacrament of confirmation, the latter of which was normally conferred during the same ceremony but which could be dispensed with by the local ordinary (see chapter 5 above). Even in 1967, the distinction between reception and the initiation rites had been underscored by the Secretariat for Christian Unity. Annibale Bugnini, archbishop secretary of the *Consilium*, records the instruction that "a profession of faith is the only act formally required for reception into the full communion of the Catholic Church."[12] The idea that reception into the church completes the rites of initiation is a novelty of the discussions, and seems to have originated in the *Consilium*. It marks a significant

12. He notes that "[T]he Secretariat for Christian Unity had decided (October 17, 1967) not to ask for any more than this." See Annibale Bugnini, *The Reform of the Liturgy, 1948–1975*, trans. Matthew J. O'Connell (Collegeville, MN: Liturgical Press, 1990), 596.

departure from the tradition, which had always judged a rite on the skin or a verbal profession—regardless of its relation to initiation—as the act which effected the entry of an already initiated (i.e., baptized) Christian to the Roman Catholic Church.

## Post–Vatican II Reforms

The first schema proposed for the reform of the Roman *ordo* for receiving baptized Christians envisioned a profession of faith, followed by the imposition of the hand, followed by confirmation for all but the Orthodox. This schema was marked by long discussions on the suitability of the imposition of hands in the act of reception. Some argued that the gesture was too connected to the rites of penance and confirmation.[13] But as noted by Archbishop Bugnini, this was "the oldest gesture"[14] associated with the reception of baptized Christians into the (Western) church. Ultimately the gesture was accepted, seen as being both an "admission into the church and remission of sins."[15] In the first schema, then, the act of reception was the imposition of hand, but later in the rite the sacrament of confirmation was also to be conferred (on all but the Eastern Christians) in order to maintain the initiatory baptism-confirmation-Eucharist order that was central to all the reforms undertaken by the *Consilium*.[16] This

13. Sieverding, *Reception of Baptized Christians*, 64.

14. Bugnini, *Reform of the Liturgy*, 596. He favorably notes a letter of Pope Innocent I (PL 20:475B) from the early fifth century.

15. Sieverding, *Reception of Baptized Christians*, 67.

16. Turner, *When Other Christians Become Catholic*, 59–60.

would change in the subsequent schemas with confirmation and reception becoming more closely tied.

The second schema called again for a profession of faith followed by the imposition of the hand and (only for the non-Orthodox) confirmation.[17] It was in this schema that the new *ordo* received its enduring name: it was now a "rite for the admission of the already validly baptized into the full communion of the Catholic Church."[18] This second schema suggested that the reception of a baptized Christian to full communion normatively would take place during the Eucharistic liturgy.[19] The schema additionally mentioned the imposition of the right hand, as in the reconciliatory gesture of the *Pontificale Romanum* of 1595.[20] The schema also suggested that only one imposition of hand take place if the candidate was to be confirmed— and thus imposition of hand now had two meanings: reception into the church and the act of confirmation.[21] This was an even more pronounced identification of confirmation with the reception than was envisioned in the first schema. With regard to the ritual structure

17. A discussion of the entire schema can be found at Sieverding, *Reception of Baptized Christians*, 72–78.

18. Consilium ad exsequendam constitutionem de Sacra Liturgia, Coetus a Studiis XXII, *Schema* 252 §1, *De Rituali* 24 (3 November 1967). For a discussion, see Sieverding, *Reception of Baptized Christians*, 72; Turner, *When Other Christians Become Catholic*, 58.

19. Coetus XXII, *Schema* 252 §8.

20. Coetus XXII, *Schema* 252 §13. For Sieverding, this rubrical note makes clear that the compilers of this schema envisioned the imposition of the hand as a penitential ritual for admission to the church. See Sieverding, *Reception of Baptized Christians*, 75.

21. Coetus XXII, *Schema* 252 §14.

and gestures, no substantial changes were made in the third schema.[22]

The fourth schema followed a similar structure but also had a clause allowing for the admission of Eastern Christians to "be done without any special rite."[23] They could now opt for just a profession of faith followed by the "act of reception" through a laying on of the hand, or for reception without a special rite. For all others being received into the church and undergoing confirmation, the structure now consisted of the reception through imposition of hand followed by the confirmation prayer with another imposition of hand. This lessened the identification of the ritual of reception with confirmation that had begun in the second schema.

The final schema, which is largely the same as the final text,[24] almost eliminated the distinction between reception and confirmation. For Eastern Christians, the schema allowed "a simple profession of faith without any special ceremony for entrance into the full

22. For a discussion, see Sieverding, *Reception of Baptized Christians*, 74.

23. Coetus a Studiis XXII, *Schema* 276 §2, *De Rituali* 26 (8 March 1968). See also Sieverding, *Reception of Baptized Christians*, 78.

24. For the final text, see the "Ordo admissionis valide iam baptizatorum in plenam communionem ecclesiae catholicae" in the appendix to *Rituale Romanum ex decreto Sacrosancti Oecumenici Concilii Vaticani II instauratum auctoritate pauli PP. VI promulgatum, Ordo initiationis christianae adultorum, editio typica* (Vatican City: Libreria Editrice Vaticana, 1972). For a discussion of the adaptations from the fourth schema, see Sieverding, *Reception of Baptized Christians*, 89–90.

communion of the Catholic church."[25] For Christians being received from the Reformation churches, however, the compilers dropped the imposition of hands during the "act of reception" (when the minister states that "the Lord receives you into the Catholic Church") if confirmation was to follow.[26] The abandonment of the first imposition was significant, since that gesture was "considered the 'act of reception' "[27]; confirmation now occupies the symbolic center of the rite. This change is deeply regrettable and has contributed to ongoing confusion about the ritual act of reception: technically, the moment of reception should still be the formula "the Lord receives you into the Catholic Church," since even for individuals coming from a church of the Reformation, confirmation can be delayed under exceptional circumstances.[28] The skin rite that is so easily psychologically understood as the ritual act of reception, however, has led to the focus being on confirmation.

In the final form, converts from Eastern Christian churches are dispensed from all but the profession of faith, though the note that the other ceremonies "may be dispensed with" suggests that there may be a scenario in which they are used. In pastoral practice, clergy often are poorly formed on how to receive

25. Coetus a Studiis XXII, *Schema* 290 §2, *De Rituali* 28 (21 April 1968). Sieverding, *Reception of Baptized Christians*, 84.

26. Coetus a Studiis XXII, *Schema* 290 §14, *De Rituali* 28 (21 April 1968).

27. Sieverding, *Reception of Baptized Christians*, 85.

28. Sieverding, *Reception of Baptized Christians*, 86. See also the "Ordo admissionis," §16–18.

Eastern Christians and at times elect to reconfirm or even rebaptize Eastern Christian candidates seeking full communion with the Catholic Church.

For Christians from churches of the Reformation, the final rite reflects the paradigm of initiation (baptism-confirmation-Eucharist). Presumably the double imposition of hands seemed redundant, and the general Catholic tendency is to prefer the sacramental to the non-sacramental form. The rite allows for an exceptional case, in which candidates are received through an imposition of hand at the act of reception without confirmation. Presumably they would then be able to receive the Eucharist. The schemas were constructed when not all priests could receive the faculty to administer confirmation.[29]

The second and normative mode of reception for Christians from churches of the Reformation is for them to receive confirmation directly after the "act of reception." This leads to only one imposition of hand in the confirmation rite itself, which now has a double meaning (reception and confirmation). This conflation of reception and confirmation does not represent the Western tradition, even in the texts that served as direct sources for the work of the *Consilium*. It also goes against the directives for the Secretariat of Christian Unity, received during the work of the *Consilium*. The *Consilium* drafters seem to have prioritized the intra-Catholic conversation on restoring the order of initiation over (a) the historical gestures used in the reception of baptized Christians in the West and (b) the ecumenical implications of the rite for the Reforma-

29. Sieverding, *Reception of Baptized Christians*, 71, 75, 77, 80, and 81–82.

tion churches. This pattern, in which a question about the relationships across ecclesial boundaries is taken by church authorities (and, indeed, lay Catholics) to be primarily important for what it says about internal Catholic debates, is one that continues to bedevil Catholic ecumenical efforts today.[30] Like the adoption of skin rites, it is an example of how the maintenance of external ecclesial boundaries is derived from and has unintended consequences for the self-understanding of the community.

The ambiguity of the gesture of reception in the final form of the current rite also muddies the conversation about Protestant confirmation.[31] In the 1993 *Directory for the Application of Principles and Norms on Ecumenism*, official Catholic Church policy acknowledges that the issue of the validity of Protestant confirmation remains unresolved. Because of this lack of resolution, the church currently requires the confirmation of every new candidate from a Protestant communion:

> In the present state of our relations with the ecclesial communities of the Reformation of the sixteenth century, we have not yet reached agreement

30. See Kimberly Hope Belcher, *Eucharist and Receptive Ecumenism: From Thanksgiving to Communion* (Cambridge/New York: Cambridge University Press, 2021), chap. 8, "The Eschatological Exception," for a contemporary example.

31. "The question of confirmation among the protestant churches that have such a ritual was not settled in the discussion after the Council of Trent (Cf. Synod of Rouen 1581), nor has it been settled to this day. To reiterate the problem, when confirmation is celebrated in the Rite of Reception, it takes on the added meaning of reception. The theological integrity of confirmation is compromised by this rite." Sieverding, *Reception of Baptized Christians*, 109.

about the significance or sacramental nature or even of the administration of the sacrament of Confirmation. Therefore, under present circumstances, persons entering into full communion with the Catholic church from one of these Communities are to receive the sacrament of Confirmation according to the doctrine and rite of the Catholic church before being admitted to eucharistic communion.[32]

However, it might be worth reconsidering whether the rite of reception to the church is really the place where such confirmations should be done. The fundamental question appears to be what lies at the heart of the reception of baptized Christians. Is it a process of initiation, or a process of reception to full communion—or both? "Completing" the initiation of candidates for full communion is counter to the Catholic Church's recognition of these candidates' initiation and the partial communion between their churches and Rome. Even though—or perhaps because—the 1993 Ecumenical Directory expresses agnosticism about the status of Protestant confirmation, confirming these Christians might imply that their initiation is incomplete. This could suggest, in turn, that the initiation of others in their communions is also incomplete. Such an interpretation would be at odds with the validation of baptism in Reformation traditions which is found in Vatican II documents.[33]

In short, the reception to full communion of Christians by confirmation makes an invalid analogy be-

32. Pontifical Council for Promoting Christian Unity, *Directory for the Application of Principles and Norms on Ecumenism* (Vatican City: Libreria Editrice Vaticana, 1993), 101.
33. For example, UR 22 and 40.

tween the "imperfect communion" shared by baptized Christians outside the Roman Catholic Church and the status of baptized Catholics who have not yet received the other two sacraments of initiation. When celebrated, as it often is, at the Easter Vigil, the present rite confuses two ceremonies (reception and confirmation) that had typically been kept distinct throughout the history of Western liturgy. Even with well-formed and well-intentioned parish practitioners, it can thus give the sense that non-Catholics who are baptized are, nevertheless, non-Christians.[34] Since the rite of reception is normally celebrated by a priest acting on the bishop's behalf, it symbolically communicates a completion of initiation (especially when used in combination with the OCIA) rather than the incorporation into a social body headed by the local bishop. The current rite of reception is therefore in need of a reevaluation.

The understanding of the reception of baptized Christians as a renewal of their baptismal identity has been broadly adopted within the mainline churches of the Reformation. There has been little scholarly study of the way that baptized Christians historically entered into communion with these traditions and of the ways that Christians changed ecclesial identities, particularly in the early period of the Reformation. In fact, most of the work done on the rites of reception in the churches of the Reformation has revolved around the rites that were constructed in the modern period.[35]

34. Maxwell E. Johnson, "Let's Stop Making 'Converts' at Easter," *Rite* 35, no. 3 (May 2004): 4–8.

35. A summary of the current rites appears in Turner, *When Other Christians Become Catholic*, chap. 6.

The Anglicans (here Church of England)[36] and Episcopalians (USA)[37] have rites of reception, in which a bishop lays hands on the candidate, saying, "We recognize you as a member of the one holy catholic and apostolic Church, and we receive you into the fellowship of this Communion. God, the Father, Son, and Holy Spirit, bless, preserve, and keep you."[38] Significantly, the *Book of Common Prayer* categorizes this rite with the ordinary rite of confirmation and renewal of baptismal vows, rather than with the rite of baptism. In the Lutheran (represented here by the Evangelical Lutheran Church in America), Methodist, and Presbyterian (Presbyterian Church USA) traditions, reception is performed with a ritual of affirmation of baptism that often includes a laying on of hands and sometimes anointing.[39] For others, like the Baptists (largely

36. See the "Reception into the Communion of the Church of England within a Celebration of Holy Communion," in *Common Worship: Christian Initiation* (London: Church House Publishing, 2015). We are indebted to Tom McLean for his lively firsthand accounts of Anglican reception rites.

37. The rite of reception is "Confirmation with Forms for Reception and for the Reaffirmation of Baptismal Vows," in the Episcopal Church, *The Book of Common Prayer and Administration of the Sacraments and Other Rites and Ceremonies of the Church: Together with the Psalter or Psalms of David according to the Use of the Episcopal Church* (New York: Seabury Press, 1979). There are also rites of preparation in "Preparation for Confirmation, Reception or Other Reaffirmations of the Baptismal Covenant," in *The Book of Occasional Services* (2018).

38. The Episcopal Church, *Book of Common Prayer*, 418.

39. For the Lutherans, see the "Affirmation of Baptism," in *Evangelical Lutheran Worship*, Pew Edition (Minneapolis: Augsburg Fortress, 2006). For Methodists, see *The United Methodist Book*

inheritors of the Anabaptist tradition), rebaptism is almost always practiced.[40] Practice among Pentecostals is widely variant, but since many of them put more emphasis on the baptism of the Holy Spirit (frequently associated with speaking in tongues) than on water baptism, reception into classical Pentecostal churches would not necessarily include rebaptism.

## Theological and Ecumenical Conclusions

It is not surprising that the question of baptism outside a church's recognized boundaries induces challenging questions about ecclesiology. After all, baptism includes incorporation into the church, an eschatological reality whose full realization is impeded by Christian disunity. All of us who have been baptized into a divided church are both fully initiated—because we participate in Christ, who is risen, whole, and glorified—and not yet fully initiated, because the fullness of reconciliation that was his mission is still

---

*of Worship* (Nashville: United Methodist Publishing House, 1992), but also the updated services, "The Services of the Baptismal Covenant in the United Methodist Church: As Revised to Align with the 2008 Book of Discipline and Book of Resolutions" (Nashville: United Methodist Publishing House, 2009). For Presbyterians, see the "Profession of Faith (Confirmation)," in Presbyterian Church (USA), *Book of Common Worship* (Louisville, KY: Westminster John Knox Press, 2018).

40. Thomas Nettles, "Baptist View: Baptism as a Symbol of Christ's Saving Work," in *Understanding Four Views on Baptism*, ed. Thomas Nettles et al., Counterpoints (Grand Rapids, MI: Zondervan, 2007), 40.

incomplete. Having been fully bound up into Christ and marked by the Holy Spirit, we nonetheless are not fully bound to one another. Our membership in Christ's body bears the visible wounds of ecclesial fragmentation. Already in 1964, *Unitatis Redintegratio* (UR) confessed that "the divisions among Christians prevent the Church from attaining the fullness of catholicity proper to her, in those of her sons who, though attached to her by Baptism, are yet separated from full communion with her. Furthermore, the Church herself finds it more difficult to express in actual life her full catholicity in all her bearings" (UR 4). Contemporary divisions wound our full participation in Christ's body, though our eschatological destiny is still fullness.

Taking this eschatological idea of the church seriously allows us to bring healing to divisions, both theologically and pastorally. Christians seeking full communion with the Catholic Church can serve as a witness to a larger image of church, a vision that reflects the mysterious majesty of a God who always exceeds our expectations. More concretely, candidates for full communion bring the distinctive gifts of their communities: in them we witness "the life of grace; faith, hope and charity, with the other interior gifts of the Holy Spirit" (UR 3). It is our privilege, in preparing candidates for reception, to recognize that "anything wrought by the grace of the Holy Spirit in the hearts of our separated brethren can be a help to our own edification. Whatever is truly Christian is never contrary to what genuinely belongs to the faith; indeed, it can always bring a deeper realization of the mystery of Christ and the Church" (UR 4). Among Eastern Christians being received, as well as (increasingly) among Western

Christians who have been influenced by Eastern spirituality, we witness to those gifts noted by UR: devotion to the sacred liturgy, hymnody and Marian devotion, monastic life, and ecclesial law and custom. Among Western Christians, we witness "a love and reverence of Sacred Scripture," often demonstrated in "constant meditative study" (UR 22), as well as the evidence of Christian life: private prayer, public worship, charity, and "a strong sense of justice," which Vatican II labels an "active faith" (UR 23). Inescapably, these gifts—and others that are not yet noted in Roman Catholic ecumenical documents—are perceptible when Christians seek to be received into a new church family.

These gifts we see in candidates for reception are not isolated, piecemeal, or accidental facts; rather, they are a witness of the full extent of Christ's church, for the church does not exist only to save individuals, but rather to serve sacramentally as a sign and instrument of God's will that all creation be restored. As *Lumen Gentium* (LG) puts it, the church is "a lasting and sure seed of unity, hope and salvation for the whole human race. Established by Christ as a communion of life, charity and truth, it is also used by Him as an instrument for the redemption of all, and is sent forth into the whole world as the light of the world and the salt of the earth" (LG 9). Our candidates for full communion often serve to us as sacramental signs that Christ and the Holy Spirit continue to nurture the seed when our attention is elsewhere, so that the harvest of the kingdom seems to spring up from the earth by its own power.[41]

41. "The kingdom of God is as if someone would scatter seed on the ground, and would sleep and rise night and day, and the

As we have seen from our historical survey, candidates for full communion have long served as a reminder that the boundaries of Christ's church are porous.

At Saint Augustine's Church and Newman Center in Gainesville, Florida, in 1999, when I (Kimberly Belcher) was received into full communion, the catechetical team was accustomed to speak of both catechumens and candidates as "sacraments" to the parish. Their sacramentality, I have since come to understand, was a direct consequence of the sacramental character of the church (LG 9): they were sacraments within the local ecclesial community to call the community to fulfill more perfectly its own essential calling. Candidates were understood as revelatory signs of the call to continuing conversion that is the ongoing gift of the Holy Spirit to the baptized. In their responsiveness to God's call, they were examples; in their particular discernments of mission, they also served as instruments of conversion for the parish as a whole. The Ecumenical Directory distinguishes the work of reception from ecumenical work to prevent our ecumenical commitments from being *reduced to* serial reception of individual Christians into Catholic communion, but this does not prevent our ecumenical work from being *informed by* the respect for our ecumenical partners we develop by seeing the faith formed in their communities.

"Baptism and Growth in Communion," the 2022 report of the international Lutheran-Roman Catholic

---

seed would sprout and grow, he does not know how. The earth produces of itself, first the stalk, then the head, then the full grain in the head. But when the grain is ripe, at once he goes in with his sickle, because the harvest has come" (Mark 6:26-29, NRSV).

Commission on Unity, describes a process of growth in communion from the "imperfect communion" (UR 4) established by baptism through a discernment of the gifts of the Spirit.[42] The document bases on Vatican II its claim that the Roman Catholic Church does not make an exclusive claim to be the church of Christ,[43] despite the way that ecclesiality "subsists in" the Catholic Church (UR 4). Our historical work substantiates and deepens this claim: both Eastern and Western churches, by their practices of reception, have always acknowledged the existence of the church outside the boundaries of their own communion. Moreover, the ecclesial gifts manifest in each communion come from eschatological participation in the mission of Christ and the Holy Spirit: "the separated Churches and Communities as such, though we believe them to be deficient in some respects, have been by no means deprived of significance and importance in the mystery of salvation. For

42. Lutheran-Roman Catholic Commission on Unity, "Baptism and Growth in Communion" (Geneva: Lutheran World Federation, 2022).

43. *"The Roman Catholic Church does not exclusively identify itself with the Church of Christ.* In a footnote, *Unitatis Redintegratio* 3 justifies the use of the term 'church' for Eastern churches. The Council addresses the other Christian communities in the West as 'Separated Churches and Ecclesial Communities in the West.' The term *communitates ecclesiales* replaces the former expression *communitates*, but the Council did not clarify which of the communities in the West may be called 'church.'" Lutheran-Catholic Commission on Unity, "Baptism and Growth in Communion," 50, emphasis original. This interpretation is controversial, as the document itself concedes: see the preface (p. 7) and the dissent in the Appendix (p. 76).

the Spirit of Christ has not refrained from using them as means of salvation which derive their efficacy from the very fullness of grace and truth entrusted to the Church" (UR 4). If they are means of salvation, then they are 'churchly,' ecclesial. "Baptism and Growth in Communion" builds on this reading of *Unitatis Redintegratio*: "if it is true that the Holy Spirit does not refrain from using certain ecclesial communities as means of grace, this discernment should then lead these communities to recognize each other as members of the body of Christ."[44]

Our growth in communion as Lutherans and Catholics can be facilitated by the mutual work of discerning together the gifts of the Holy Spirit: recognizing in one another the way the Holy Spirit is at work in the whole Body of Christ. Of course, not all candidates for full communion are Lutheran; nonetheless, the principles of this document should be applied to our understanding of reception. "The fruit of the Spirit is God's gift to ecclesial communities and to every believer in order to make present the Gospel and to mediate God's grace,"[45] such that our recognition of the fruits of the Spirit and the virtues of faith, hope, and love in candidates for full communion should be witness of the Spirit's work in other communities.

> *Discerning the fruit of the Spirit requires criteria.*
> *Lutherans and Catholics utilize basically the same*

44. Lutheran-Catholic Commission on Unity, "Baptism and Growth in Communion," 54.

45. Lutheran-Catholic Commission on Unity, "Baptism and Growth in Communion," 53.

*ones.* They agree that every prayer, teaching, and action which creates and expresses faith, hope, and love, which opens the ears and hearts for the Word of God, which builds up the church, and which deepens communion with Christ and communion between believers and communities is a true fruit of the Spirit. Each gift is given by God in order to build up others and the whole church (1 Cor 12:4-7). This "building up" of others and the church is the main criterion Catholics and Lutherans need to identify and actualize at this time.[46]

It would be an aid to our ecumenical commitments to recognize that receptive ecumenism includes reception, and that by means of reception we have the opportunity to receive also the gifts the Spirit has bestowed for the sake of the world on our ecumenical partners. Rather, we are already receiving those gifts, and we have a responsibility, then, to recognize them. By so doing we make progress toward the most difficult ecumenical task: the discernment of unity *in* (not despite) legitimate difference: "even if the Holy Spirit communicates God's saving Word through differing doctrine and practices of another community, these differences in doctrines and institutional forms can be seen in a new light if one also takes into consideration that they are means to bring forth the fruit of the Spirit that we can observe in the other community."[47]

46. Lutheran-Catholic Commission on Unity, "Baptism and Growth in Communion," 53–54.

47. Lutheran-Catholic Commission on Unity, "Baptism and Growth in Communion," 54.

A pertinent example is how chrism is envisioned in different but complementary ways by the Eastern and Western churches. Among its many functions in the Eastern churches, chrism is tied to the legitimate episcopal hierarchy, and for each Christian, receiving the patriarch or bishop's chrism is essential for the complete celebration of Christian initiation. In the West, on the other hand, confirmation and by extension chrism is not necessary for the belonging of individual Christians. The touch of the bishop's hand on the head of a Christian was a normative way of understanding the biosocial integration of the ecclesial body, but it was not absolutely necessary to have been touched by a bishop to be fully initiated. The chrism and the handlaying in the West are in a way proleptically implied even in the water bath, just as is communion.[48] This difference accounts for the different development of chrismation in East and West. It also demonstrates one way that the current rite of reception is an ecumenical double standard: it seems to imply that Protestant baptisms need to be completed with confirmation before communion, while Catholic baptisms do not. Since the Reformation churches inherited the Western Christian tradition, it is understandable that handlaying plays a larger role than chrismation in their initiatory practices.

48. "By Baptism [one] is ordained to the Eucharist, and therefore from the fact of children being baptized, they are destined by the Church to the Eucharist; and just as they believe through the Church's faith, so they desire the Eucharist through the Church's intention, and, as a result, receive its reality." Thomas Aquinas, *Summa Theologica*, IIIa, 73, 3, respondeo. On confirmation, see ST IIIa, 72, 1, ad. 3; IIIa, 72, 2, ad. 4.

If the mutual recognition of baptism is to be fully made manifest, we must recognize that the longstanding conflict between theology and practice is not merely the result of ignorance. Rather, it reflects the need, especially in small, marginalized, or vulnerable communities, to amplify the group's sense of identity by strengthening its boundaries. Elaborate rites, especially on the skin of those who are to be initiated, strengthen a group's sense of security and solidarity at the expense of the full recognition of Christians in other churches. The current issues could be resolved by a clarification between the bishop's imposition of hands (reception) as a mode of ecclesial location and the use of hand-laying and chrism (confirmation) as a renovation and completion of baptism.

Even before the twentieth century and the modern ecumenical movement, the central authorities in East and West have historically prioritized recognizing one another's baptisms and ecclesial status. The social pressure to differentiate oneself from the other, however, often led to a struggle to implement these ecumenical policies at a local level. This challenge continues, and is one primary reason for the difficulty of ecumenical reception. Local investment in our ecumenical commitments is inhibited by resistance identities against other local Christian groups (especially those that are perceived as more dominant). This resistance is often overcome by local experience working with other Christians for an immediate need, discovering on the way their shared faith in Jesus and recognizing a shared life in baptism. This often happens in shared work for peace or poverty relief, but in learning to accompany candidates for reception and in appreciating their baptism and Christian formation, we can also practice local ecumenical conversion. In these experiences, local communities that might be prone to emphasizing their boundaries are instead permitted to be converted toward a more ecumenical identity.

The Groupe des Dombes describes such a conversion, in which Christians as individuals, as confessions, and as a whole church are transformed into a stronger likeness of Christ. The document distinguishes confessionalism from confessional conversion as ways of identifying and valuing one's tradition and its distinctive features. Confessionalism derives its identity from its contrast with other churches, seeking opportunities to divide and ways that other traditions are lesser. Confessional conversion also identifies distinctive elements of one's own church, but chooses gifts that have the potential to unite the churches more closely. Confessional conversion, then, is a process of discernment that turns toward those distinctive gifts that amplify our love for other Christians and our longing for unity, and leaves behind our resistance identities that rejoice in our separations.[49] Ecumenism does not mean the eradication of difference, but the weighing of differences against Christ's call to Christian unity (John 17:20-24).

In the spirit of confessional conversion, the Roman Catholic Church needs to revisit the benefits of the baptism-confirmation-Eucharist paradigm in the reception of baptized Christians. The *Consilium*'s desire to recover from the early church the pattern of initiation that culminates in the Eucharist motivated them to "re-

---

49. Groupe des Dombes, *For the Conversion of the Churches* (Geneva: World Council of Churches Publications, 1993).

store the order," whenever possible, of confirmation before communion. Of course, at that moment it seemed possible that this would become universal Catholic practice, which has not been the case. This paradigm, which was intended to renew Roman Catholic sacramental thinking, instead was imposed on candidates for full communion but *not* restored in general Catholic practice. This is one of a number of situations in which the Roman Catholic Church has been more focused on possible consequences for its own internal life than on very clear consequences for its relationships with others—a temptation for central communities.[50]

Candidates for reception already have an unusual initiatory pattern, which cannot be conformed to a baptism-confirmation-Eucharist pattern; it is more important that their reception contribute to the greater unity of Christians in Christ.[51] The mid-century interest in restoring a pristine initiatory pattern, the universality of which is now much more doubtful, identified

50. For other examples, see Belcher, *Eucharist and Receptive Ecumenism*, chap. 8.

51. The need for negotiation of such conflicts between different potential benefits is foreseen in UR 11: "The way and method in which the Catholic faith is expressed should never become an obstacle to dialogue with our brethren. It is, of course, essential that the doctrine should be clearly presented in its entirety. Nothing is so foreign to the spirit of ecumenism as a false irenicism, in which the purity of Catholic doctrine suffers loss and its genuine and certain meaning is clouded. . . . When comparing doctrines with one another, they should remember that in Catholic doctrine there exists a 'hierarchy' of truths, since they vary in their relation to the fundamental Christian faith. Thus the way will be opened by which through fraternal rivalry all will be stirred to a deeper understanding and a clearer presentation of the unfathomable riches of Christ."

reception with a renewal of baptism. This theology is not problematic: indeed, the emphasis on renewal of baptism, through the shift toward an Eastern understanding of chrism in confirmation, is received in the liturgical books of many mainline Protestant churches. At the same time, the initiatory pattern is much less important than our recognition of authentic baptism and ecclesial belonging across community boundaries. Historically, the laying on of hands is the clearest gesture for receiving baptized Christians into the Catholic Church, despite the fact that a distinct reception by the imposition of hands was eliminated from the final version of the current ritual. Current Roman Catholic documents are clear that being a member of another church does not make one a sinner, heretic, or schismatic; moreover, since they are recognized as members of Christ, their initiation, with whatever handlaying or anointing it includes, is true initiation. The reception of Christians from the churches of the Reformation using penance, confirmation, and Communion is at odds with our recognition of the ecclesiality of these communities in our documents, and prematurely resolves the question about the validity of Protestant confirmation. These ecclesiological issues are more important than a normative order, not only in contemporary theological reflection, but even in the historical record.

The current ritual conflates reception and confirmation. Moreover, those who are candidates for full communion generally receive sacramental reconciliation before they have actually been received into communion with the church, even though those not in full communion are in most circumstances not eligible for sacramental penance. Requiring reconciliation implies, wrongly, that there is inherent sin in being separated from the Roman Catholic Church. Requiring confirmation at least suggests that Protestant baptisms are incomplete and less sufficient for receiving communion than Catholic baptism. We will suggest a reform of this rite. At the same time, there are practices permissible under the current books that would help to bring the celebration of the reception of baptized Christians into line with official church teaching. We will turn to these first.

## Best Practices Using the Current Liturgical Book

The best practices for receiving baptized Christians under the current ecclesial books have two parts: the formation of those to be received and the celebration of the rite of reception.[52] We will propose revisions to the rite of reception below, but the rite cannot be changed unilaterally by episcopal conferences, let alone by pastoral ministers. Instead, it must be changed by the institutional processes at the highest level of ecclesiastical authority—those in the relevant dicasteries of

---

52. For a number of best pastoral practices ranging from respect for baptism to the best way to celebrate the various parts of the rites, see Ronald A. Oakham, ed., *One at the Table: The Reception of Baptized Christians*, Font and Table Series (Chicago: Liturgy Training Publications, 1995), part 2. This is largely repeated, but in a different form and with some further reflection on the rite of reception itself in Ronald A. Oakham, *The Reception of Baptized Christians: Pastoral and Practical Approaches* (Chicago: Liturgy Training Publications, 2020). For best practices on formation, see David Yamane, Sarah MacMillen, and Kelly Culver, *Real Stories of Christian Initiation: Lessons for and from the RCIA* (Collegeville, MN: Liturgical Press, 2006).

the Roman Curia. This section seeks to address what pastoral ministers can or should do *now* given the options that are available to them. There is no one-size-fits-all approach to how to receive baptized Christians; however, the following pastoral recommendations are informed by the history of the reception of baptized Christians and the theology of the rite.

The first pastoral recommendation is that in all things, the formation of baptized Christians who express interest in being received into the Catholic Church must be grounded in our respect for their baptism. This will, for many candidates for reception, mean working against their inclinations. They may be disappointed that they have already been baptized, either because they do not remember it, or because they disdain the tradition they were baptized into. Pastoral judgment will be needed to help candidates discern, in their own call narrative, the work of the Holy Spirit active within their communities of origin—and, on the other hand, to release them from any elements of spiritual unfreedom they received from those communities. This will entail distinguishing between the work of the Holy Spirit in their traditions and the sinful systems they may have experienced within those communities. This discernment is a sacramental sign to the Catholic Church, which also experiences the need to distinguish in its own communal life between the work of the Holy Spirit and structures of sin. Pastoral judgment exercised in this context would benefit from teaching explicitly the sacramental ecclesiology of reception outlined in the previous section.

The ecumenical service of walking with candidates for reception will mean doing ecumenical work alongside candidates to value the baptisms of communities whose theology divides them from us, and in some cases who have hurt the candidates or their families, or who may be prejudiced against Catholics. The foundation for this work is the same as it has been since Augustine: baptism belongs to Christ alone, and transcends the minister who baptizes. Acknowledging this is already an act of ecclesial humility: the good gifts we offer in initiation come from Jesus, and we are at best honest stewards. As a result, it is also crucial that the formation and the ritual practice of reception avoid triumphalism, as the rite itself says, and affirm the communion we already have by virtue of our baptism (UR 4).

The respect for the baptism of the individual being received will be best accomplished, where pastoral resources permit, if the formation and act of reception of baptized Christians are done apart from the OCIA. The reception of baptized Christians should clearly be distinguished from the OCIA because those being received have already become members of the Body of Christ through their baptism. As a result, the reception of baptized Christians does not really belong with the OCIA, and just because it currently is placed in the *editio typica* and vernacular translations of the OCIA does not mean that it has to be treated as part of the OCIA in terms of formation and liturgical celebration. Those in charge of formation and the implementation of the reception of baptized Christians should in all things distinguish between the rite of reception and the OCIA. At the same time, the OCIA can provide some guidance on how to construct a formation program for individuals being received and even provide inspiration for liturgical rites that can mark their formation journey.

In terms of their formation, the rite of reception is clear that the individual's circumstances must be taken into account when determining the formation they need and when they should be initiated. In other words, candidates' needs and preparation should be carefully assessed by those in charge of their formation, and a formation program should be constructed that attends to the needs of each individual being received. For some, especially those who are clearly already well educated in the faith, this formation may be minimal and the duration of the formation may be quite short. But for most individuals being received, they will likely need a good deal of formation on the Catholic tradition and even of Christian doctrine, and so the duration of their formation program may be more substantial.

In general, a program of formation that combines catechesis with some form of mystagogy will be key. The mystagogical component, in particular, can help individuals come to appreciate their baptism, by helping them interpret the baptism they received in their churches of origin as well as in their life of faith so far. The contrast of their tradition of origin with the Catholic faith should never be exaggerated; whatever coherence it exhibits should be honored, and its distinctive emphases that have contributed to the candidate's faith journey should be highlighted and respected. These individuals, in particular, bring unique gifts to the Catholic Church that come from their churches of origin. These gifts must be shared and cherished.

Whether this formation program is done in conjunction with those in formation in the OCIA or not will ultimately be up to the needs and resources of each local parish. Ideally, those being received will be formed in their own community apart from those in the OCIA (at least for most of their formation program). However, uncatechized adults who are undergoing formation for confirmation are, in fact, better suited as formation companions for those being received than those undergoing the OCIA. Other adults in the parish who are interested in learning more about their faith might also find formation with candidates for reception to be both theologically and ecumenically fruitful. Like those being received into the Catholic Church, uncatechized adults preparing for confirmation should ideally be formed in a program separate from those undergoing the OCIA. Pastoral separation of these groups will also allow the formation of candidates for reception or confirmation to be done throughout the liturgical year (see more below). An added benefit of bringing these groups together is that each can contribute their own gifts and experiences to the other. Often those to be received into the Catholic Church have a deeper catechesis and Christian formation than those Catholics in the parish community whose catechesis has been "neglected." This is especially true of their scriptural knowledge and formation. This can provide rich insights to the uncatechized adults in the program preparing for confirmation.

However, not every parish will be able to create separate formation programs for those in the OCIA, those to be received into the Catholic Church, and uncatechized adults seeking confirmation. In those instances, parish formators must work extra hard to ensure that distinctions between each group are maintained. There may even be reasons to bring these groups together for occasional formation sessions, even in parishes where the number of individuals going through these rites, as well as the number of formators and resources, allows for distinct formation programs for these groups. Each of these groups brings their own experiences and gifts. The sharing of those experiences and gifts can be mutually enriching.

Theologically, throughout the formation of those to be received, formators should not force the rite into a paradigm of initiation or reconciliation. Throughout the history of the rite of reception, we have seen the way the rite of reception has sometimes been interpreted as a completion of initiation, sometimes as an act of reconciliation, and at other times as something in between. Like any ritual within the Christian ritual system, the rite of reception contains liturgical and theological dimensions and connections to other parts of the Christian sacramental and ritual tradition. In this way, the rite of reception has deep connections to the rites of initiation and the rite of penance. It also contains theological connections to healing rites and is often connected pastorally to the sacrament of marriage; many of those undergoing the rite of reception are doing so in order to be married in the Catholic Church. The theological and pastoral connections to the other sacraments and rituals within the Catholic liturgical tradition should each be raised up. The connection to the individual's baptism, for instance, is especially important. However, it should be clear that the rite of reception is not a rite of initiation: rather, it is a rite of welcome into and belonging within the Catholic communion. Though it may be experienced as a renewal of baptism, this should be seen as a constant call to conversion that is key to the

Christian call to holiness, and not a sign of a deficiency in the community of origin.

Part of the desire to interpret this rite within either an initiatory or reconciliatory framework is the desire on the part of many to have meaningful religious moments in their lives marked by a sacrament. In the rite of reception and other rituals within the Christian tradition, this way of thinking must be avoided. Not every important ritual in a Christian's life needs to be a sacrament. The rite of reception is significant on its own terms; it need not be conceptualized or experienced as a sacrament. Its own proper significance should be stressed to those being received. After all, it is the reception of the Eucharist that sacramentally manifests the fullness of "full communion," and the ritual performance should communicate this clearly.

The need to distinguish between those going through the OCIA, the rite of reception, and preparation for confirmation is not limited to the formation programs they are in; it extends to the liturgical rites themselves. Clear liturgical distinctions between these groups would strengthen not only the identity and self-understanding of the members of each of these groups, but also the broader parish community. There are several places in the OCIA where each of these groups can be brought together liturgically under "combined rites":

1. Rite for Entrance into the Catechumenate and of Welcoming the Candidates

2. Rite of Sending Catechumens for Election and Candidates for the Calling to Continuing Conversion

3. Rite of Election of Catechumens and of Calling the Candidates to Continuing Conversion

4. Celebration at the Easter Vigil of the Sacraments of Initiation and the Rite of Reception

While expedient, each of these combined rites is also pastorally problematic, given that many participants do not see the subtle distinctions articulated in the rites between the catechumens and both sets of candidates (those undergoing the rite of reception and those preparing for confirmation). In fact, there were some concerns raised about the combined rites before they were finally approved.[53] As a result, the rites themselves note that "care must be taken to maintain the distinction between the catechumens and the baptized candidates" (506). Interestingly, there is little distinction given in the rite to the two groups of baptized candidates, those being received and those preparing for confirmation. This is a deficiency in the rites that should be addressed in formation.

The use of the first two rites (#1 and #2) is determined at the parish level; they may be used or they may not be used. If rites of entrance and sending are desired by the parish community, it is likely best that these be done separately for those in the OCIA, on

---

53. Dale J. Sieverding, *Ordo admissionis valide iam baptizatorum in plenam communionem ecclesiae catholicae: An Historical Study of the Ritual Aspects of Reception into Full Communion with Special Attention to the Adaptations of the Rite for Use in the Catholic Church in the United States of America*, SLD diss. (Rome: Pontifical Liturgical Institute, 1997), 279–80; Sieverding, *Reception of Baptized Christians*, 102–3.

the one hand, and those being received or undergoing confirmation on the other. As a result, the separate form of the rites given should be used.

The Rite of Election of Catechumens and of Calling the Candidates to Continuing Conversion (#3) is often determined by the local ordinary. As such, parishes may not have much say in whether the combined or separate rites are used. When possible, it would be desirable if the bishop did not use the combined rite. Travel concerns could be addressed by two separate rites on the same day in a single diocese. For those parishes that are in a diocese where the combined rites are used, clear formation ahead of the celebration of the rite is needed.

Finally, the use of the combined rite at the Easter Vigil (#4) is again up to the discretion of the parish. Just as with the other combined rites, the combined rite at the Easter Vigil can blur distinctions between those undergoing the OCIA, those being received, and uncatechized adults preparing for confirmation. The introduction to the combined rite makes these issues apparent in paragraphs 564 and 565 (in the current ritual books), which draw attention to the requirement that those being received into the Catholic Church be received according to their individual need. It also indicates that those being received are already part of the Body of Christ by virtue of their baptism. The need for them to be consulted on the manner of their reception, and for that reception to be consistent with the Catholic Church's ecumenical values, is also noted in the introduction.

Besides the combined rites' lack of clear differentiation in practice between those in the OCIA, those being received, and uncatechized adults preparing for confirmation, the downside of these combined rites from the perspective of those undergoing the rite of reception is that they do not allow individuals to be received when they are ready. Part of the challenge with constructing a formation program and even celebrating the rite of reception is that the instructions call for individuals to be received when they are deemed ready. The combined rites, more than anything, force those undergoing reception to be received primarily at one time in the liturgical year, namely the Easter Vigil. This does not respect their own formation journey. At the same time, logistically many parishes can only run one formation program for those in the OCIA, those being received, and those preparing for confirmation. Furthermore, there may even be clear pastoral reasons (for example, a family being received and baptized together) to use the combined rite. Ideally, however, there would be several times throughout the year for individuals seeking to be received, and even for uncatechized adults interested in being confirmed, to enter formation programs and be received. It does not seem unreasonable for there to be a formation program that runs in the fall during Advent, leading up to a celebration during the Christmas season (perhaps at Epiphany), and another in Lent, leading up to a celebration within the Easter season.

Those forming individuals being received into the Catholic Church may also find it useful to mark their period of formation with a number of liturgical celebrations. Inspiration for these services can be drawn from the OCIA, in particular the celebrations of the word of God. These celebrations might provide a good model for those being received, as well as for uncatechized adults going through formation for confirmation. Some of these celebrations of the word of God, especially those celebrated in conjunction with catechesis, might be celebrated with the catechumens as long as those being received and the uncatechized adults going through formation for confirmation do not receive the optional minor exorcisms given for the catechumens. However, a special blessing for their formation and preparation for the celebration of the rite of reception would be especially appropriate.

Throughout their formation, their baptism can be ritually commemorated, for instance, in the use of the Creed and the Lord's Prayer, in the sign of the cross and the use of holy water, and in renewing their baptismal vows and calling them to continual conversion. Rites of baptismal renewal might be practiced while they are in formation, a process which should not be prolonged more than is needed. Those being received into the Catholic Church should also be encouraged to frequent Eucharistic celebrations and to stay for the whole liturgy. In the OCIA, catechumens are frequently dismissed before the liturgy of the Eucharist begins. This ritual discipline, retrieved from fourth- and fifth-century liturgical documents, manifests to the catechumens the holiness of the Eucharist and the importance of baptism to membership in the church.[54] Candidates for reception, however, are baptized, and as such should not be dismissed from the Sunday

54. Kimberly Hope Belcher, "Adiaphora and Inscription: Ritual Fiction and the Disciplina Arcani in the Fourth Century," in *Explorations in Christian Initiation from the East: In Honor of Maxwell E. Johnson*, ed. Stefanos Alexopoulos, Nathan Chase, and Anna Petrin, Eastern Catholic Studies and Texts (Washington, DC: The Catholic University of America Press, forthcoming, 2025).

assembly. They are proper partakers in the universal prayers, the thanksgiving of the eucharistic prayer, and the sign of peace. The common celebration of the Liturgy of the Hours is also to be commended.

Like with the formation of uncatechized adults who are preparing for confirmation, it may also be appropriate to utilize some of the other rites within the OCIA as well, like the Rite of Handing On of the Creed, the Rite of Handing On of the Lord's Prayer, or the Presentation of the Gospels. Formators may also adapt the Rite of Welcoming the Candidates used for uncatechized adults who are seeking confirmation, as well as the Rite of Sending the Candidates for the Calling to Continuing Conversion and the Rite of Calling the Candidates to Continuing Conversion. However, the prayers should be refashioned for those being received into the church, and they should not be dismissed from the assembly. Care should also be taken to make sure that the penitential rite done as part of the formation of those who are being received into the Catholic Church as well as in that of uncatechized adults seeking confirmation makes a clear distinction between these different groups of candidates.

After their reception, it would be tremendously beneficial if individuals participated in the period of mystagogy outlined in the OCIA. While this period is primarily geared toward the neophytes, all of the faithful are encouraged to participate in this mystagogical reflection on the rites of initiation in the Easter season. This is especially the case for uncatechized adults who were confirmed, but also for those who were received into the Catholic Church. In fact, since those being received have already undergone baptism, it would be good to do mystagogical reflection with them throughout their formation.

Concerning the rite of reception itself, there are a number of best practices that are worth raising up. The first is found in the instructions to the rite itself, namely that those being received should be consulted on the manner in which the rite is celebrated. It is especially important, given that many being received may have family and friends from different churches present—including the individual's church of origin—that the rite be celebrated in a way that is ecumenically sensitive and avoids any air of triumphalism. In this way, the reception of baptized Christians would become more closely connected with our ecumenical relationships, not by way of "sheep-stealing," but by way of discernment and the mutual exchange of gifts.

In this rite of reception, appropriate Scriptures, including those associated with the work of Christian unity, should be read. Those presiding over the rite of reception should also consider making use of the provision in the rite to use the readings and prayers for the Mass for the Unity of Christians. This can be a very powerful ecumenical statement. In the homily, the homilist would do well to focus in particular on the importance of baptism, ecumenism, and the importance of this rite as a welcome into the Catholic Church. The universal prayer should also be tailored to the experience of the one being received and should also express a spirit of ecumenism.

## Toward a New Liturgical Rite

In conclusion, we suggest a new service for receiving baptized Christians that is shaped by history and which also takes into account many of the best practices described above. We should not initiate Christians from churches of the Reformation by the sacrament of reconciliation, which restores communion with the church broken through grievous sin, since in their case full communion has not begun and they bear no responsibility for the historic breach of communion. Rather, the reception rite should be an imposition of hands by the bishop or his representative priest, as is the general pattern in the Western ritual tradition. At that point, having been received into the Catholic communion, they are eligible communicants. We are recommending that absolution be made part of this rite as an extraordinary preparation for communion, with private confession deferred until they have been received into communion. If it is necessary for them to receive the sacrament of confirmation as the "completion" of initiation, newly received Catholics should be confirmed at a later date—perhaps with other *confirmandi* in the local church. There are already plenty of baptized Catholics living in the church globally despite a so-called "incomplete" initiation—those who have been baptized, that is, but who have not yet received confirmation and/or the Eucharist. This would include most Catholics under the age of fourteen or so, a normative time for confirmation, but also a large number of adult Catholics who have, for a variety of reasons, not proceeded with their sacramental preparation.

For Eastern Christians not in communion with Rome, the current rite requires simply a profession of faith, which respects the historical tradition in the East and West of receiving different ecclesial groups based on their ecclesial proximity. However, one of the challenges in pastoral practice is that categorical distinctions between ecclesial groups quickly break down and seem ambiguous. Thus we hear many anecdotes in which Catholic pastors choose to receive Eastern Christians by confirmation or even rebaptism, even though this is explicitly forbidden. As we have seen, such anomalies have a long history.

While the profession of faith is all that is required, therefore, we recommend using the same ritual of reception for Eastern Christians and for individuals coming from the churches of the Reformation. This would entail a laying on of hands, which emerges from our study as the historical ritual gesture most oriented toward receiving a baptized Christian into the Catholic Church. It is also a meaningful and welcoming gesture that dignifies a Christian's reception into full communion but does not repeat any of the valid sacramental practices of Eastern or Western Christians. It would retrieve and lift up the importance of touch—specifically in the form of the imposition of hands—to establish ecclesial belonging in the Western tradition. This approach would allow, for the first time, for a single ritual act of reception that is theologically coherent in its distinction from the normative course of initiation as well as consistent in its application across ecclesial circumstances.

Looking beyond the rite of reception to the whole formation process for those being received, we feel that a new introduction should spell out the best practices described in the section above for the formation of those being received into the Catholic Church. It should also include a more detailed account of the liturgical rites that may mark the formation of those being received. Here again we feel the introduction can take inspiration from the best practices described above, as well as from the rites given in the OCIA for the catechumens and for uncatechized adults seeking confirmation. In the interest of space, and wishing for the expertise of others, particularly formators, we will not make any changes to the introduction that touch on the formation process for those being received.

While we are Roman Catholic liturgical scholars, we believe that our dialogue with history and respect for the Eastern churches also justify some reflections on the Byzantine liturgical tradition. It is worth noting that from the time of the First Ecumenical Council (I Nicaea) until 1756, non-Orthodox Christians who had been baptized into the Blessed Trinity were normatively received into the Eastern Orthodox Church after an anathema of their "heresy" and the anointing with holy chrism (*myron*/μύρον). Both in its liturgical rites and among its theologians, the Byzantine Church prior to 1484 also stipulated that the anointing of baptized converts was the liturgical means for curing "heresy," thus for incorporating baptized but separated Christians into the church. Another historical concern for a few Orthodox theologians, but which appears nowhere in the rites of the ancient Byzantine Church,[55] was the particular

---

55. In the Greek-speaking East, the major theological exemplars are the fourth-century reflections of Didymus of Alexandria, *De trinitate* 2.15, PG 39:720–21; and the twelfth-century account of Niketas of Nicomedia, whose words were reported during a post-1054 theological debate in Constantinople by Anselm of Haverberg, *Dialogi* 3.21, PL 188:1246–47. Additionally, two important medieval canonists mention, in passing, this motive for anointing baptized converts: John Zonaras, *Commentary on Apostolic Canon 47*, in Σύνταγμα τῶν θείων καὶ ἱερῶν κανόνων, vol. 2, ed. Georgios A. Ralles and Michael Potles (Athens: Chartophylakos, 1852), 62; Matthew Blastares, *Al-*

requirement for using chrism because an anointing with chrism was an essential part of the baptismal rites.

In light of the consistent belief and practice of the Byzantine Church, then, the ritual anointing of a baptized convert has a dual function which distinguishes it from an act which might be thought to "complete" an ostensibly incomplete Christian initiation. On the one hand, it was sociologically analogous to the Western Church's use of hand-imposition to receive baptized converts: it served as a rite on the skin by which the central community reinforced its self-identity in regard to its ecclesial boundaries. On the other hand, it emerges from the undivided church as an ecumenically sensitive liturgical rite for receiving converts in the midst of the current divisions among Christians.

Of course, it is not necessary for East and West to have comparable processes for reception, as indeed has rarely been historically the case. It seems to have been relatively unproblematic for each church to evaluate the others' practices against their own understanding of baptism. At the same time, a full or even partial reappropriation of the Byzantine approach—in the style of a "ressourcement"—has much to offer to the

------

*phabetical Syntagma* 2.1, in Σύνταγμα τῶν θείων καὶ ἱερῶν κανόνων, vol. 6, ed. Ralles and Potles (Athens: Chartophylakos, 1857). In Slavic Orthodoxy, the idea is much more ubiquitous, having originated in the seventeenth century with the ostensibly "Westernized" sacramental theology of Peter Moghila. For a discussion of these approaches, see John H. Erickson, "The Reception of Non-Orthodox into the Church: Contemporary Practice," *St. Vladimir's Theological Quarterly* 41 (1997): 4–7; Klentos, "Rebaptizing Converts," 226–29; Nicholas E. Denysenko, *Chrismation: A Primer for Catholics* (Collegeville, MN: Liturgical Press, 2014), 46, 87.

contemporary situation in the Orthodox churches of ritual and theoretical variety with respect to receiving baptized converts. Among other concerns, this provides the possibility of developing a theology of reception that focuses on (1) ecclesial reconciliation rather than the completion of initiation; (2) the healing of an ecclesial wound rather than the forgiveness of a sin against doctrine; and (3) a liturgical recognition of the sharing among churches of the one divinely instituted baptism.

What follows is a proposed new *ordo* for the reception of baptized Christians into the Roman Catholic Church that takes as its starting point the current rite of reception. As argued throughout this chapter, the current "rite of reception of a validly baptized Christian to full communion" (appendix to the Latin *editio typica* of the OCIA) is in drastic need of reevaluation. Symbolically speaking, the current *ordo*'s use of rites on the skin is confusing at best. Sooner rather than later, the rite should undergo a further liturgical reform, which would allow it to function not within the OCIA as a merely pastoral rite, but as an authentic expression of our ecumenical commitments. This would also allow it to function as a distinct ritual in the Catholic Church, unshackled from some of the problematic connections to initiation and penance that we have seen in its history. The proposed rite is intended to more effectively distinguish the ecclesial, liturgical, and ecumenical implications of its gestures and words. While intended for study purposes only, this proposed rite is based on the historical, theological, and ritual findings of this book. It is hoped that it might inform future revisions to the current rite of reception in the OCIA.

Appendix

# A Proposed Order of Reception into the Full Communion of the Catholic Church of Those Already Validly Baptized

## For Study Use Only

This ritual, proposed for study and discussion toward an eventual revised rite of reception, is adapted from "Order of Reception into the Full Communion of the Catholic Church of Those Already Validly Baptized," OCIA 473–504. Texts quoted verbatim are noted as such in the Commentary.

| Introduction | Commentary |
| --- | --- |
| **1** The rite by which a person born and baptized in a separated ecclesial Community is received into the full communion of the Catholic Church according to the Latin Rite,[1] is so arranged that no further burden is imposed than what is necessary to restore communion and unity[2] (cf. Acts 15:28). | *This is quoted verbatim from OCIA 473.* |
| **2** Nothing more is required of Eastern Christians coming to the fullness of Catholic communion, however, than what a simple profession of Catholic faith requires, even if, by virtue of recourse to the Apostolic See, a transfer to the Latin Rite is permitted to them.[3] Only a simple profession of faith is required, but ordinarily the following rite should be used as a way to solemnize their profession of faith. | *The first half of this paragraph is quoted verbatim from OCIA 474. However, in order to create consistency across the reception of baptized Christians, it would be of benefit to the Church if Eastern Christians being received into the communion of the Catholic Church would do so through the more solemn ritual, though this is not required.* |

1. Cf. Second Vatican Council, Constitution on the Sacred Liturgy, *Sacrosanctum Concilium*, no. 69b; Decree on Ecumenism, *Unitatis redintegratio*, no. 3; Secretariat for Christian Unity, Ecumenical Directory I, no. 19; *Acta Apostolicæ Sedis* 59 (1967), p. 581.

2. Cf. Second Vatican Council, Decree on Ecumenism, *Unitatis redintegratio*, no. 18.

3. Cf. Second Vatican Council, Decree on Eastern Catholic Churches, *Orientalium Ecclesiarum*, nos. 25 and 4.

**3** In regard to the manner of celebrating the Rite of Reception:

a) The rite of the celebration should appear as a celebration of the Church, and its high point should be realized in Eucharistic Communion. Therefore the admission normally should take place during Mass. The Mass for the Unity of Christians can be substituted for the Mass of the day, provided the Rite of Reception does not take place on a Sunday of Advent, Lent or Easter, or on any solemnity,[4] or another suitable votive Mass may be used.

*3.a is quoted verbatim from OCIA 475a with the exception of the addition of the Mass for the Unity of Christians, which seems a particularly suitable Mass for this ritual context.*

b) Liturgical practices that give an air of triumphalism in the rite of Reception should be avoided. At no point should those being received be asked to abjure the teachings of their former tradition, nor should it be implied that their communities are heretical. The way in which this Mass will be celebrated must be attentive to pastoral circumstances. Both ecumenical commitments and the bond

*3.b is adapted from the existing rite.*

4. Cf. *The Roman Missal*, 3rd ed. (2011), "Masses and Prayers for Various Needs and Occasions," 17.

between the candidate and the local church should influence its celebration. Although a celebration within a Mass is preferable, Reception may be held outside Mass if there is a serious reason. If possible, Reception should be celebrated at least within a Liturgy of the Word. The person being received should assist in choosing the form of the Reception.

c) The rite should be celebrated at a time which will allow those in need of confirmation to receive it at a later date with the other candidates for confirmation in the parish or local church.

*3.c is a new addition. In an effort to separate the rite of reception from the celebration of confirmation, the proposed* ordo *now calls for the rite of reception to occur at a time which will allow individuals in need of confirmation to receive it with other members of the parish at a later date.*

d) The rite should not be celebrated at the Easter Vigil or in combination with the *Order of Christian Initiation of Adults* (henceforth OCIA) or an ordinary celebration of confirmation.

*3.d is a new addition. In order to prevent confusion between those undergoing the OCIA, confirmation, and reception, it is best that those being received be received at a separate celebration. This affirms the dignity of their baptism and allows them to be received when they are ready, instead of waiting for the Easter Vigil.*

| | |
|---|---|
| **4** If Reception is celebrated outside Mass, its connection with Eucharistic Communion should be made clear by having it followed as soon as possible by a Eucharistic Celebration, in which the newly received fully participates among Catholic brothers and sisters for the first time. | *Quoted verbatim from OCIA 476.* |
| **5** For the Reception of those already baptized into the full communion of the Catholic Church, both a doctrinal and a spiritual preparation of the candidate is required, according to pastoral needs accommodated to individual cases. A candidate should learn to adhere more and more lovingly to the Church, in which the candidate will find the fullness of his or her Baptism.<br><br>At the time of this preparation some sharing in worship may already be taking place, according to the norms established in the Ecumenical Directory.<br><br>Equating candidates with catechumens is to be altogether avoided. | *Quoted verbatim from OCIA 477.* |

| | |
|---|---|
| **6** During their preparation period, candidates for Reception into full communion may benefit in their formation from the celebration of liturgical rites. For this purpose, one or several of the rites included in the OCIA chapter V—"Preparing Adults for Confirmation and the Eucharist Who Were Baptized as Infants and Did Not Receive Catechesis"—may be celebrated or adapted to better reflect their pastoral needs and their relationship with the local community. The length of catechetical formation needed by each individual candidate for Reception into full communion should be discerned by the candidate and the pastoral team. | *Adapted from the current rite.* |
| **7** An abjuration of heresy is no longer required of a person who was born and baptized outside the visible communion of the Catholic Church, but only a profession of faith.[5] | *Quoted verbatim from OCIA 479.* |

5. Cf. Secretariat for Christian Unity, Ecumenical Directory I, nos. 19 and 20: *Acta Apostolicæ Sedis* 59 (1967), 581.

8 The Sacrament of Baptism cannot be repeated, and therefore conditional Baptism is not permitted to be conferred again unless a prudent doubt is present concerning the fact or the validity of the Baptism already conferred. If after a serious investigation has been undertaken concerning the prudent doubt about the fact or validity of the Baptism already conferred, conditional Baptism seems necessary to confer again, the minister should appropriately explain the reasons why Baptism in this case is being conferred conditionally, and he should administer it in a private form.[6]

The local Ordinary should determine in individual cases of conferring conditional Baptism which rites should be kept and which omitted.

9 It is for the Bishop to receive the candidate for Reception. A priest, however, to whom he entrusts the celebration to be performed, has

*Quoted verbatim from OCIA 480.*

*The first part of this section is adapted from the existing rite. Clarification about confirmation is included here as well to conform it to 3.c and the*

---

6. Cf. Ecumenical Directory I, nos. 14–15: *Acta Apostolicæ Sedis* 59 (1967), p. 580.

the faculty of receiving the candidate. Confirmation is no longer celebrated during the Rite of Reception for anyone entering into the communion of the Catholic Church except in danger of death and other exceptional situations outlined by the local Ordinary. If confirmation is required, the rite (cf. OCIA 231–235) is to be inserted between no. 23 and 24 with no alterations to the Rite of Reception.

*desire to create a distinction between the rite of reception and the sacrament of confirmation.*

**10** The one being received does not confess his or her sins in individual confession before the forthcoming Reception, since they are not yet part of the Catholic Church. Instead, the Rite of Reception serves as a rite of ecclesial reconciliation and includes general confession and absolution within the rite itself drawn from the *Order of Penance* (no. 20). The individual(s) being received should go to individual confession as soon as they have the opportunity and within a year of their Reception.

*This section is thoroughly revised. The rite of reception itself contains an act of general absolution and the candidate to be received is to go to individual confession after their reception. It is ecclesiologically problematic for an individual to receive the sacrament of reconciliation when they are not yet part of the Catholic Church. Additionally, this draws attention to the way historically the rite of reception has also had reconciliatory and penitential dimensions.*

**11** If the situation warrants, a sponsor, namely a man or a woman who had a greater role than others in leading or preparing the candidate, may accompany the one being

*Quoted verbatim from OCIA 483.*

admitted in the Reception itself; two sponsors may also be
permitted.

**12** In the Eucharistic Celebration itself during which the Reception takes place, or, if this
happens outside the solemni-
ties of the Mass, in the Mass
that follows, it is permitted
not only for the one admitted
to receive Holy Communion
under both kinds, but also the
sponsors, parents, spouse (if
these are Catholic), lay cate-
chists who perhaps instructed
the one being received, and
indeed all Catholics present, if
their number or other circumstances suggest it.

*Quoted verbatim from OCIA
484.*

**13** The Rite of Reception may
be adapted to various circumstances by the Conferences
of Bishops according to the
Constitution on the Sacred
Liturgy (no. 63). Above all the
local Ordinary, paying attention to special conditions of
persons and places, may himself adapt the Rite to them, by
expanding or abbreviating it,
if it seems appropriate.[7] The
local Ordinary or Conference
of Bishops may not change the
act of Reception (no. 22).

*This section is quoted verba-
tim from OCIA 485 with the
exception of the last sentence.
A review of the history shows
that the laying on of hands is
historically the act of reception in the West. The local
ordinary is not permitted to
change this gesture.*

---

7. Cf. Secretariat for Christian Unity, Ecumenical Directory I, no.
19: *Acta Apostolicæ Sedis* 59 (1967), p. 581.

**14** The names of those received should be recorded in a special book, along with the date and place of their Baptism.

*Quoted verbatim from OCIA 486.*

## ORDER OF RECEPTION WITHIN MASS

**15** On a Solemnity or a Sunday, Reception should be celebrated within the Mass of the day; on other days, the Mass for the Unity of Christians or another suitable votive Mass may be used to reflect the candidate's spirituality or his/her bond with the local community.

*Adapted from the current rite. Votive Masses that speak to the individual's spirituality (e.g., the Mass of the Holy Spirit) may be appropriate.*

## LITURGY OF THE WORD

### READINGS

**16** The biblical readings for Mass may be taken in whole or in part from those provided in the *Lectionary for Mass* for the Mass of the day, from the Mass for the Unity of Christians (cf. nos. 867–71), or from another suitable votive Mass.

*Adapted from the current rite but with the omission of the option to use the readings for the Ritual Mass for Christian Initiation Apart from the Easter Vigil and the addition to use other votive Masses. Again, this is an attempt to distinguish the rite of reception from initiation.*

HOMILY

**17** The Reception is carried out after the Homily, in which the celebrant, with gratitude to God, should speak of Baptism as the basis for the candidate's Reception and of the Most Holy Eucharist, to be celebrated by the candidate for the first time with the Catholic community.

*Quoted from OCIA 489, omitting the reference to confirmation.*

CELEBRATION OF RECEPTION

INVITATION

**18** After the Homily, the celebrant, in these or similar words, invites the candidate with his/her sponsor to approach and profess his/her faith:

N., since after mature deliberation in the Holy Spirit
and of your own free will
you have asked to be received
into the full communion of
the Catholic Church,
I now invite you to come forward with your sponsor
and in the presence of this
community,
[confess your sin, renew your
baptismal promises,
and] profess the Catholic faith.

*This is adapted from OCIA 490, but the phrase "confess your sin, renew your baptismal promises," has been added to remind the candidates and the assembly of the importance of their baptism and to foreshadow the act of general confession and absolution that will occur in the rite.*

In this faith, today for the first
time
you will partake with us at
the eucharistic table of the
Lord Jesus,
by which the unity of the
Church is signified.

## RENUNCIATION OF SIN

**19** Then the person to be received is to renounce sin.

At your Baptism you re-
nounced Satan and all sin. But
we have all fallen short of our
baptismal promises. Today
you will renew your baptismal promises and confess
your sins.

Do you renounce sin, so as to
live in the freedom of the children of God?

I do.

Do you renounce the lure of
evil, so that sin may have no
mastery over you?

I do.

Do you renounce Satan, the
author and prince of sin?

I do.

*This addition to the rite mir-
rors a renewal of baptismal
promises, again in order to
accentuate the importance of
baptism, and to prepare for
the act of general absolution.
These questions and responses
are quoted verbatim from
OCIA 224.*

GENERAL ABSOLUTION

20 Then the person to be received is invited to kneel or bow, and to acknowledge sin:

Acknowledge the sins you have committed since your Baptism and receive God's pardon.

Do you acknowledge the sins that you have committed?

I do and I confess that I have greatly sinned. May almighty God have mercy on me, forgive me my sins, and bring me to everlasting life.

The celebrant then gives absolution, holding his hands extended over the person to be received and saying:

God, the Father of mercies, through the Death and Resurrection of his Son
has reconciled the world to himself
and poured out the Holy Spirit
for the forgiveness of sins;
through the ministry of the Church
may God grant you pardon and peace.
And I absolve you from your sins,
in the name of the Father, and of the Son, +
and of the Holy Spirit.

*This has been added to the rite in order to rectify the ecclesiological issue of reconciling an individual who is not yet part of the Catholic Church. It is adapted from the* Order of Penance. *Candidates for reception may reply with any suitable confession and expression of contrition.*

*This formula for absolution is quoted verbatim from the* Order of Penance, *no. 46.*

The candidate for Reception replies:
Amen.

## PROFESSION OF FAITH

**21** After absolution, the celebrant, in these or similar words, briefly invites all to renew their Baptism through the recitation of the Niceno-Constantinopolitan Creed:

Having heard the renunciation of sin and confession, we all join now in renewing our baptism by professing the words of the Nicene Creed.

Then the person to be received, together with the faithful, recites the Niceno-Constantinopolitan Creed, which is always said at this Mass. If the candidate came from an Eastern Christian tradition, the *filioque* clause ("and from the Son" in the article on the Holy Spirit) may be omitted.

After this, at the celebrant's invitation, the one to be received adds:

I believe and profess
all that the holy Catholic Church
believes, teaches, and proclaims as revealed by God.

*The profession of faith is a logical extension of the request for forgiveness. The references to the renunciation and confession of sin are additions to the text. The possible omission of the* filioque *clause for those coming from an Eastern Christian tradition is an attempt to be sensitive to their concerns, especially since it is preferable that they undergo this rite. All of the rest is adapted from the existing rite.*

*This expression of the candidate's intent is quoted verbatim from OCIA 491.*

## ACT OF RECEPTION

**22** The celebrant then lays his right hand upon the head of the person to be received and says:

N., the Lord receives you into the Catholic Church.
In his mercy he has led you here,
so that in the Holy Spirit you may have full communion with us
in the faith you have professed before this his family.

### Prayer for the Newly Received

Lord God almighty, Father of our Lord Jesus Christ,
guard in N. closely his/her faith in you,
forgiving him/her all his/her sins,
and increasing in him/her your righteousness.
Send onto him/her, Lord, the holy Paraclete,
the spirit of wisdom and understanding,
the spirit of counsel and fortitude,
the spirit of knowledge and piety,
and fill him/her, Lord, with the Spirit of God,
in the name of Jesus Christ, our saving God,

*The formula of the act of reception is quoted verbatim from OCIA 492. References to confirmation, which in this proposed revision is not ordinarily meant to follow, have been removed.*

*This prayer is our translation of the traditional Western prayer used for the rite of reception. (Sacramentarium Gelasianum I.LXXXV; see p. 64) but with the addition of a line from the traditional Byzantine prayer for reception as well. The goal was to make this prayer more ecumenically sensitive.*

| | |
|---|---|
| through whom and with whom<br>all honor and glory is yours<br>for ever and ever.<br>Amen. | |
| **CELEBRANT'S SIGN OF WELCOME**<br><br>**23** After the act of Reception the celebrant greets the one newly received, taking his (her) hand between his own hands to welcome the candidate into the Catholic Church personally, on behalf of the assembly, and as a representative of the local Bishop. The local Ordinary may identify another suitable gesture, depending on pastoral need and local norms. | *Adapted from the existing rite. If confirmation is to be celebrated, it is to be placed after this sign of welcome, which concludes the rite of reception, and before the universal prayer which begins the movement toward the celebration of the Eucharist.* |
| **UNIVERSAL PRAYER (PRAYER OF THE FAITHFUL)**<br><br>**24** The Universal Prayer follows the Reception. In his introduction the celebrant should mention Baptism and the Eucharist, and express gratitude to God. The person received into full communion is mentioned at the beginning of the intentions. If confirmation is celebrated, it may be included in the petitions. | *Adapted from the existing rite, where examples of petitions can be found.* |

| | |
|---|---|
| SIGN OF PEACE<br><br>**25** After the Universal Prayer (Prayer of the Faithful) the sponsor and, if there are only a few persons, all who are present may, if appropriate, greet the newly-received person in a friendly manner. In this case the Sign of Peace before Communion may be omitted. Finally, the person received returns to his (her) place. | *Quoted from OCIA 497.* |
| CELEBRATION OF THE EUCHARIST<br><br>**26** Then the Mass continues. It is fitting that the person received and the others mentioned in no. 12 above receive the Most Sacred Eucharist under both kinds. | *Quoted from OCIA 498.* |
| ORDER OF RECEPTION OUTSIDE MASS<br><br>**27** If, for a serious reason, the Reception takes place outside Mass, a Liturgy of the Word is celebrated.<br><br>If, due to extraordinary circumstances, it appears that the Reception is to be celebrated without the Liturgy of the Word, everything takes place as above in nos. 18–23, | *Quoted from OCIA 499.* |

| | |
|---|---|
| beginning with the celebrant's Instruction (no. 18). This Instruction should begin with a quotation from Sacred Scripture, for example, a text that praises the mercy of God that has led the candidate to be received into full communion and speaks of the Eucharistic Communion soon to be received at a later time. | |
| **28** The celebrant, wearing an alb, or at least a surplice, and a stole of festive color, greets those present. | *Quoted from OCIA 500.* |
| **29** The celebration begins with a suitable chant and a reading of Sacred Scripture, which is explained in the Homily (cf. no. 17).<br><br>The biblical readings may be taken in whole or in part from those provided in the *Lectionary for Mass* for the Mass of the day, or for the Mass for the Unity of Christians (cf. nos. 867–71), or from another suitable votive Mass.<br><br>When the rite, however, is celebrated outside Mass, it is preferable that the texts that follow be used (cf. *Lectionary for Mass*, nos. 761–63). | *Quoted from OCIA 501, but with the omission of the option to use the readings for the Ritual Mass for Christian Initiation Apart from the Easter Vigil in order to distinguish the rite of reception from initiation. Instead, the readings from another suitable votive Mass may be used.* |

| | |
|---|---|
| **30** Then follows the Reception, to be carried out in the manner described (nos. 18–23). | *Quoted from OCIA 502.* |
| **31** The Universal Prayer follows the Reception as described in no. 24. In his introduction the celebrant should mention Baptism and the Eucharist, and express gratitude to God. The person received into full communion is mentioned at the beginning of the intentions. | *Adapted from the existing rite.* |
| **32** The Universal Prayer is concluded with the Lord's Prayer, sung or recited by all present.<br><br>The celebrant introduces the Lord's Prayer, in the following or similar words:<br><br>Dear brothers and sisters, let us unite our prayers and offer them, praying as our Lord Jesus Christ taught us:<br><br>All:<br>Our Father . . .<br><br>If the person received was accustomed in his (her) Community to the final doxology For the kingdom, etc., it should be added here to the Lord's Prayer. | *Quoted from OCIA 504.* |

| The celebrant's blessing follows. Then the sponsor and, if there are only a few persons, all who are present may, if appropriate, greet the newly-received person in a friendly manner. After this, all then depart in peace. | |
|---|---|

# Index

**Table of Figures**